THE WHISPERED RAGA

By
Sudipto Roy Choudhury

This edition is published by BecomeShakespeare.com in 2015
in India, Sri Lanka, USA and UK

This is a work of fiction. Names, characters, businesses, places, events and incidents are either the products of the author's imagination or used in a fictitious manner. Any resemblance to actual persons, living or dead, or actual events is purely coincidental.

First published in 2015 by

BecomeShakespeare.com
Wordit Content Design & Editing Services Pvt Ltd
Quest Offices, C38/39,
Parinee Crescenzo Building, G Block,
Bandra Kurla Complex, Bandra East,
Mumbai 400 051, India
T: +91 8080226699

Copyright © 2015 by Subroto Roy Choudhury

All rights reserved. Any unauthorized reprint or use of this material is prohibited. No part of this book may be reproduced or transmitted in any form or by any means, electronic or mechanical, including photocopying, recording, or by any information storage and retrieval system without express written permission from the author/publisher.
Please do not participate in or encourage piracy of copyrighted materials in violation of the author's rights.
Purchase only authorized editions.

ISBN 978-93-83952-31-1

Three kinds of souls, three prayers: I am a bow in your hands, draw me lest I rot.

Do not overdraw me, I shall break. Overdraw me; who cares if I break.

— *Nikos Kazantzakis*

There is music everywhere in this world, and those who can drink of its joy are blessed.

— *Ustad Bare Ghulam Ali Khan*

I came who knows where

To hear the words from her lips.

But my efforts were in vain,

I didn't hear, couldn't hear her.

I returned home and now I hear,

Hear her words in my ears.

The person of my heart is in my heart…

— *Rabindranath Tagore, after traditional Baul songs*

For Pandit Kumarprasad Mukhopadhyay, doyen of
Bengali writers on North Indian classical music

And

To my *dadu* Ganga Charan Mukherjee and my late father
Dulal Roy Choudhury for introducing me to this world

AUTHOR'S NOTE

Besides telling the story, the four parts of the book seek also to create four different *rasas* or moods, much like the four parts of a *khayal*. Of these, part 1 is really an introduction or *alaap*, while part 2 (*Majh*) is already impending crisis and so is dramatic in structure and execution. Part 3 is the resulting flashback to the past and so like the *asthayi* or base of a *raga*. This part is emotional and very different in mood from the drama and tension in part 2. Part 4 of course is the climax where the various conflicts and crises come to a head, as the strands of a *raga* come to a crescendo in the *tarana*.

CONTENTS

Prelude: Ithaca, New York, 1995 — p. 11

1. Alaap (Introduction): Calcutta and Shantiniketan, 1974 — p. 17

2. Maajh (Middle): Ithaca, New York, 1995 — p. 105

3. Asthayi (Composition): Lucknow, Calcutta and Kanpur, 1957-74 — p. 163

4. Tarana (Crescendo): Calcutta and India, 1996 – 1998 — p. 241

5. Notes and Acknowledgments — p. 284

PRELUDE

Ithaca, New York, 1995

I could not know then how that day was to transform my life, and that of my two dearest friends. Is there a design in such things? Some flow of energy, of some mysterious life force, perhaps what people term destiny. Are we marionettes in the hands of some master puppeteer? Or merely random waves in an ocean of chance?

I wake up with a start that morning. The telephone is ringing. Who can it be at this unearthly hour?

The voice on the other end says, 'It's Guruji, Aniket. Did I wake you up?'

'Yes, Guruji,' I reply, yawning and rubbing my eyes. 'What is it?'

'It's going to work, *beta*. We've managed to fit Ithaca into the itinerary.' Guruji sounds excited as he continues, 'We'll be there two nights. So there'll be time for concerts on both evenings. Thanks a lot for arranging it, *beta*.'

'Of course, Guruji. It's the least I can do for the school,' I say. 'On what days will it be?' I am beginning to feel a bit more alert now as the implications of his words sink in. I get up and stretch, nestling the receiver between my head and right shoulder. Then I reach for the notepad lying on the bedside table – the nightstand – as it's called in the US.

'Sometime in mid-December, *beta*,' Guruji's disembodied voice responds. 'I'll let you know the exact days as soon as I know.'

'And I'll try and publicise it as much as possible in the surrounding area. It'll be so great to see all of you again after so many years.' I scratch my pot-belly. The grey spots beginning to speckle the image of my beard in the mirror trigger a rush of thoughts. Will this reunion really be unalloyed pleasure? How much have we all changed? What will the others look like after all these years? Will it still feel like old times?

'I won't be able to come this time, *beta*,' Guruji says. His voice grows slightly hoarse as he continues, 'I'm getting to be too old. Idanbai's ailing too, and it'll be too much of a strain for her. But Sureshwari may be there.'

'And who else Guruji?' I reply, probing. Inwardly, I am hoping against hope that there will be someone else.

'Well, Mr. Madan will be there, of course, representing the school in the capacity of Director. And Nazrul and Niloy as the two star male vocalists.'

'And Sureshwari Devi will be the only female singer?' I say a bit gingerly. I am still probing, hoping that his answer will be negative. Hoping that a certain person will also be coming along.

Guruji notices the hesitancy in my words. 'Our female star Rita Mahalanobis will be there, Aniket. And Lopa as well. Things aren't what they used to be at the school though, *beta*. It's a whole new world here in India.'

'But Lopa's in Lucknow, isn't she?'

'She's returned to us from Lucknow earlier this year to take care of her mother – Idanbai's sinking quite quickly.'

I say nothing. Noticing my silence, he continues quickly, '*Beta*, you will be together – Nazrul, Lopa and you – after many years. Things aren't going well for them either, Aniket. I'm sure that Nazrul will tell you when you meet.'

'But I'm helpless, Guruji. I tried what I could, and it didn't work. I'm tired, Guruji.'

'Yes, I always anticipated this, *beta*. Somehow, I knew that it would come to this. Success comes with a price, *beta*. People at the school talk about you, you know. But I've always sensed that just being an academician would never be enough for you.'

'Yes, Guruji. Everything seems flat, meaningless, tasteless. It's like everything that once gave me pleasure has lost its flavour.'

There is a long silence at the other end. Then Guruji says, '*Beta*, listen to yourself. Let yourself go. You've been performing, doing, running a race for too long. You've always done what was expected of you. But life isn't just accomplishment. Just let yourself go.'

'But what will I listen for, Guruji? Everything's dull. I wake up every morning with a feeling of dread. How do I get through the day? I'm seriously considering counselling or therapy.'

'*Beta*, I've known you since you were as high as the *tulsi* plant in my garden. Your therapy is inside you.'

'But how do I find it, Guruji? I'm at my wit's end, almost like my mind's about to give up on me. That I'm going to go mad, sink into some kind of serious depression.'

'I tried to warn you, *beta,* when you made your choice all those years ago. But listen, *beta*. Do you remember the story of the whispered *raga* I told you those many years ago?'

'Yes Guruji.'

'Well, listen for it, *beta*. Listen for it now as if your life depends on it. It's fainter now, as it is for so many people in this new world of ours where everything's external, and people run after so many things. You've become unused to even thinking of it. But it's still sounding – somewhere between the Earth and sky, it's still there waiting to fill you up with its song.'

'I don't know how, Guruji. God knows I've browsed through everything I could think of, from Jungian analysis, to psychotherapy, to pop psychology and meditation.'

'*Beta*, don't force things. This is a period of waiting and of listening. Remember what it says in the Bible – "there is a season to sow, and one to reap." This is a season for you to lay fallow. To rest. Perhaps, just to do whatever you want for some time.'

'Yes Guruji.'

'It may seem very hard *beta*. You're so used to doing things. And American culture is one of doing, isn't it?'

'Yes. Relentless, endless doing. Like being on a treadmill.'

'Well, *beta*, listen to this old man. And *beta*.'

'Yes Guruji?'

'While you're waiting, sing. Sing, *beta*. Sing as if your very life depends on it. Sing to the universe. That is your greatest gift. There's no greater medicine for such things than music, *beta*. Listen to this old man who's seen the power of music to heal.'

'But I can't even bring myself to, Guruji.'

'I know you find it hard. I know you probably don't even believe me. But keep trying, *beta*. When the time is right, when you've listened enough, then you will hear it, will find what you need.'

'I will, Guruji,' I say without much conviction in my voice. After I hang up the phone, I walk over to the window. I do not know how long I stand there staring out moodily, thinking of Guruji's words. At some instant, unbeknownst to me, my thoughts take flight on the wings of memory. Back into the past. Very far back, two whole decades, in fact. All the way to the time when fate rolled the dice that inexorably put me on the path I have travelled ever since.

ALAAP (INTRODUCTION)

Calcutta and Shantiniketan, 1974

Some are mad for riches,

Some about themselves,

Some because they haven't enough,

Some for the form,

Some for the taste;

Some are mad in love.

Some just cry and laugh

Madness has many forms.

Everyone says, "Mad, mad."

Is it the fruit of a tree?

— traditional *Baul* song

1.1

The giant navy blue letters on the lighter blue metal background of the signboard hanging above the large gate read 'Sursagar School of Music'. On the wall beneath, someone has scrawled the incongruous-sounding translation 'Ocean of Music'.

'Funny how the same phrase can sound natural in one language and pompous in another,' I think as I duck into the doorway.

A whiff of fresh jasmine hits my nostrils as I walk up the pathway. And then, I hear the familiar sounds emanating from the rehearsal rooms lining the long, sky-blue verandahs wrapped around all sides of the three-storey school building – here a *tabla* being lightly tapped by a skilfully aimed stainless steel hammer, there the atonal rasps of some old instrument's tuning keys being tweaked, or, in yet another corner, some student's attempted vocal flourish trailing off into an abrupt silence, cut short no doubt by a teacher's earnest injunction.

And then, from the far end of the second floor, in that voice which never fails to make my heart flutter, come the strains of the famous *thumri Ka Karun Sajni, Aaye na Baalam*. A few more minutes and I have pushed open the door of the room.

In the middle is the singer Nazneen, known to one and all by her nickname Lopa. Flanking her is her mother, the well-known Idanbai, her aquiline features and dark, *surma*-lined eyes now squinted into a strongly disapproving expression, and looking like a wounded serpent about to strike. There is no sign at all of the pensive, ethereal beauty which normally strikes everyone who comes into her presence even before they notice her transparent simplicity and warmth.

The school's other star female singer, Sureshwari Devi, is standing in the centre of the room agitatedly addressing a massive figure dressed in an immaculate white pyjama-kurta embroidered with borders in the Lucknow *Chikan* style. 'But what a girl you've chosen this time, Kishan-*bhaiya*! The daughter of a courtesan, a *tabaif*, a *baiji*. At your age and with your status! What will people say? That you've lost your head over a *gaanewali chhokri* in your old age.'

My mouth falls open in shock, even as the name she utters triggers recognition of the man she is addressing as the Kathak maestro Kishan Maharaj. I have never seen this side of Sureshwari Devi. The ongoing cold war between the two stars is widely discussed in the school, but no one I know has ever seen it so publicly displayed, at least not since my arrival at the school. Sureshwari's whimsical, self-centred tantrums and predatory nature, although familiar to school insiders, are usually kept well-hidden behind a suave, sophisticated exterior. Indeed, her charm is a byword among the legions of her admirers.

Even as Lopa's face turns ashen and the smile freezes on Kishan Maharaj's face, Idanbai steps forward. In a surprisingly mild tone, she says, 'We fought over Kishan many years ago, Sureshwari – twenty years ago in Bombay when we were all so young. I know that that's what still bothers you so much. *Lekin jaane do*. No matter.'

Then, turning to the dancer, she says, 'But let me show what this great lady, Kishan, what this *tabaif* can still do.

Whatever you express through your face and dance, I'll match that *bhav* through my singing.'

I see a smile begin to curl up the corners of Siddheshwari's lips. 'Kishan Maharaj's miming and expressions, the *bhav* and *abhinaya* of India's greatest Kathak dancer, and this Idanbai would rival it in song!' I can feel her thinking to herself.

Perhaps sensing a heaven-sent opportunity to defuse the tension, Kishan Maharaj needs no further prompting. He motions to Lopa, and, as they jointly launch once again into *Ka Karun Sajni Aaye Na Baalam*, he resumes the peerless miming that has made his *bhav batlana* a legend across North India.

I have begun humming the *mukhda*, the primary refrain, under my breath as they sing, with the *sa* of the upper octave as the *sam* or tonic. And then, as Lopa takes over the refrain completely, Idanbai chimes in, in her famously mellifluous and weighty voice, with the refrain beginning at the *pa* and in a completely different melody. As she returns to the *mukhda* after a particularly melodious ornament (*harkat*) on the preceding lyrics, I feel every hair on my body rise as my pores tingle with gooseflesh all over.

The alternating exposition of song and *bhav batlana* that follows takes me far beyond any musical experience I have ever known, into some mystical realm of the ineffable. With each of Kishan Maharaj's expressions, Idanbai exclaims 'Aha! Aha!', and then the tears roll from his eyes as the next phrase emerges from her mouth. They are goading each other to go ever higher, and it seems that they have reached some realm of divine melody and dance, a mythical *gandharva-*

loka. They both then burst into tears and cry profusely, and the tears soon roll down Lopa's and my cheeks as well. Only Sureshwari Devi seems unmoved, sitting in a corner, distant and unsmiling.

Eventually the singing and dancing stop, perhaps because it is humanly impossible to sustain this pitch of emotion for very long. For a few minutes, there is a hushed silence. Even Sureshwari Devi has been startled into a temporary submission.

For me, it has been an unprecedented revelation. I realise at that instant that such realms are inaccessible by mere practice, that such attainment, this fabled *swar-siddhi* which I have just been blessed to witness, is a miracle, a product of the rarest confluence of good luck and what can only be called grace.

As the atmosphere in the room returns to normal, I see Sureshwari Devi's face regain its habitual mask of inscrutable, sophisticated politeness. Then, as she stands and opens her mouth to speak, the silence is shattered by the sounds of commotion near the front gate of the school.

We all hurry out, Idanbai, Kishan Maharaj, Sureshwari Devi, Lopa and myself. We find our Guruji, Pandit Vishnu Joshi, his face flushed, standing next to a *tonga*. Guruji is loudly berating the driver, which, given his Maharashtrian Brahmin courtesy, is uncharacteristic of him. 'You scoundrel! How dare you flog these beasts of God so mercilessly? What are you, a human being or a *kasai*?' – A butcher – 'I have a good mind to give you a sound thrashing, so you'll know how it feels. Don't you know that the same spirit that lives in you is in them too?'

'But *saab*, it's just my job,' the driver says with a tart smile and with not even a hint of contrition on his face. 'Beasts of God you call them, *saab*. They're dumb but as stubborn as mules. Only the whip gets their attention.'

By now, a crowd has gathered at the scene. Some urchins from the roadside tea shop are smiling mischievously, digging their elbows into each other's sides as they gesture towards the *tonga* driver. The driver raises his right hand as if to strike them. He curses under his breath. Then, as one of the urchins brings forth an old rag and wipes off the sweat from the haunches and frames of the sweaty animals, he shouts, '*Saale, bahut mazaa aa raha hain, hain na? Jaa, bhaag yahaan se!*' ('Scoundrels, you're having a lot of fun, aren't you? Go, get lost!')

Guruji appears to calm down a bit once he catches sight of Sureshwari, Idanbai and the rest of us. Motioning to the driver of the *tonga*, he says, 'I told him to drop me at home in the *tonga*. Because it's a Sunday, and the police wouldn't be around to catch him, the rascal has whipped these horses almost black and blue. Wait here, you scoundrel, till I return!'

Without another word of explanation, he crosses over to the famous Bhim Nag sweet shop on the other side, returning a few minutes later with four large bundles wrapped in conical, dried leaf containers. Then, as I look on with a mixture of astonishment and amusement, he proceeds to remove the leaf lids and take out a kilo of piping-hot *jalebis*. He blows on them to dissipate the heat, and feeds them to the first horse, repeating the process for each of the other animals, caressing their sweaty flanks and whispering affectionately into their ears. The creatures nuzzle up to him, gobbling up the tasty treats, one huge gulp at a time. By now, even Sureshwari Devi's face is wreathed in smiles.

When this solicitous feeding is complete, Guruji turns towards the driver once more. The man's earlier air of surliness and amused insouciance has vanished completely, and he now seems all but ready to melt into the dust. 'Be gone!' spits Guruji. 'Whip a helpless animal, will you? Let this be a lesson to you. If I ever catch you at it again, I'll break that whip on your back!'

Then, turning away from the hapless man and towards the entrance, he adds, 'Come on, everyone, let's go in. It's touching noon. There're only four weeks left for the festival, and still many arrangements to be completed. And I'm going to Bombay next Monday for a couple of weeks.'

1.2

It is later that afternoon. I have come to Dhakuria Lakes with my former schoolmate, and dearest friend, Sureshwari Devi's son Nazrul. An upcoming singer from Delhi, Prem Kishan, belonging to the legendary singer Ustad Faiyaz Khan's famous Agra *gharana*, school, has accompanied us. He is visiting the school for a month to obtain *taalim* from Sureshwari Devi, and the grapevine is abuzz with talk of how he is sure to astound everyone at our annual musical festival with his vocal pyrotechnics.

I have known Nazrul since we were eleven and classmates in St. Xavier's School. Through his mother, he belongs to a *khandaani* or familial Islamic musical heritage stretching back to the last days of the Mughal Empire. And although he seems to have inherited a great deal of his mother's talent, it is hard even to imagine two people otherwise so contrary in character and temperament.

The wind is rippling the surface of the lake as we settle down on the benches near the water's edge. It strikes me as I see Prem settling down next to Nazrul that they look a bit like Laurel and Hardy. The slightly-built Nazrul with his dreamy eyes and cowlick drooping down the middle of his forehead. And hulking beside him the tall, broad-shouldered Prem Kishan. As Prem straightens his *kurta* over his powerful frame, I am reminded of the stories of the massive build of the legendary revolutionary Bagha Jatin, rumoured to once have slain a tiger with his bare hands.

Two groups of young men, probably belonging to some school or college rowing team, are plying their oars mightily and churning the water into countless reddish eddies as they criss-cross the stretch of water in front of us. The dreamy winter sun is turning the stalks of the swaying palms on the bank into liquid gold, and the gongs of the Buddhist Temple which flanks the lake are pealing in the distance.

The usual *pheriwallas* are loudly hawking everything, from cigarettes and newspapers, to delicious *bhelpuri* whose pungent aroma tantalises our noses each time a vendor walks past.

'If you don't mind my asking, Nazrul,' Prem Kishan ventures, 'how come you have the obviously Islamic name Nazrul, while your mother's named Sureshwari?'

Before Nazrul can respond I jump in. 'Come on! Why does everybody ask this question? He's a little tired of explaining this over and over again, you know.'

'All right, why don't you tell me instead?' Prem says as he rises from the bench.

'His great-grandfather was the legendary Bahram Khan, and he named his granddaughter, Nazrul's mother, Sureshwari, after the goddess Saraswati. He studied the Hindu scriptures during his youth in Banaras as part of his music training. He would even apply *chandan* – sandalwood paste – to his forehead and recite the evening prayers, but he wouldn't actually enter temples.'

'Now, that must really have been something in those days,' says Prem Kishan.

'Oh, it was. When his training was complete, he confessed to his guru in Banaras that he was Muslim, and begged his forgiveness for having deceived him. But, far from cursing him, his guru embraced him and blessed him. He remained a Krishna devotee all his life.'

'Like our Faiyaz Khan.'

'Yes. And he was liberal in other ways as well. Even in those days, he would take on poor and talented students from outside the family for free, and would reveal all the musical riches of our lineage to them.'

Nazrul is smiling. As he so often does, he has been watching the sky, and he now joins in, 'Enough about my family. See those Siberian cranes flying so beautifully in formation? They fly in every year around this time, just as the weather here becomes gorgeous. I'm always astonished at how they all know exactly when to wheel around in perfect alignment, even if each is just following a neighbour who leads the whole flock. And how does each know exactly which neighbour to follow?'

'There're many more at the zoo,' I say.

'Let's go there next week for a picnic,' says Nazrul. 'And perhaps to the Agri-Horticultural Gardens as well. Their annual flower show is on and there'll be hundreds of fruits and flowers on sale and display. Not to mention the birds which come to the small lake there during this time.'

'I think Prem Kishan might enjoy a trip to Shantiniketan even more. He was asking me about the music of the *baul* singers. They'll be out there later this month for the *Poush Mela*. That's the big annual fair they hold every winter, Prem, usually over the Christmas week,' I add, rising too and turning towards our visitor.

'Now that is a great idea,' Prem Kishan says. 'But we'd have to go mid-festival. The festival starts on the twenty-third, right, and I have to return to Delhi as soon as it's over. How about it?'

Nazrul and I look at each other in silent agreement. 'Let's do it,' Nazrul says. 'It'll also be a relief, letting off some steam during the pressure cooker atmosphere of the festival. You know, just by getting away for a day.'

'We'd better check with your mother, though,' I say. 'And with Guruji. It'll still be before our program. They may object – say that it'll affect our voices. You know, the usual sort of thing.'

'All right, but let's convince them and go anyway,' says Nazrul, barely concealing the glee in his voice. 'We can take the morning super-fast express to Bolpur. And that'll still give us time to attend the programs at the *Amro Kunjo* – that's the mango grove, Prem. And then go for the *baul* and other programmes at the main fair.'

We are interrupted by a hissed whisper behind our ears announcing, 'You want good girl? Take your pick sir – Nepali, Bengali, Bihari, Gujarati, South Indian. Or up-country sir – very fresh.'

We see Prem Kishan break into a smile. 'Not so different from Delhi, *yaar*, even in this beautiful location and in this city of Bengali *babus*.' Returning to our conversation, he says, '*Amro Kunjo* is *Amra Kunj* in Hindi too, *yaar*. Except we don't put marbles in our mouths before speaking.'

Then, a spirit of mischief seems to take hold of him. He puts his hands on his hips, and rolls his lips into a big circle. Leaning forward towards me and playing on both the legendary sweet tooth of Bengalis, as well as what sounds, to the North Indian ear, like their rounding out of all the vowels into 'oh', he clowns, *'Bongoli baboo, roshogolla khabo.* Mouth full of marbles, pebbles, and *shondesh*, na?'

The sudden switch has caught us a bit unawares but, noticing our smiles, he continues, 'Paw-tay-tow cheeps, phood in freeze. Want to hear a Bong joke guys?'

We nod, and he continues, 'How did the Bong engineer direct the vater under the breeze,' pronouncing water and bridge in typical Bengali fashion.

We smile and shake our heads. 'Give up? D'you give up?' Prem asks with the enthusiasm of a five-year old dying to spill the beans on his newest joke. 'D'you want to know?'

'OK, OK.'

'He dammed the bhaves of the oshaan so they passd obhaar filds and bhalleys and then deerected them aandar the breeze.'

We smile as he guffaws loudly at his own wit. Then Nazrul responds, 'Hey, hey. Not so fast my Punjabi friend. There is no meyyar to my pleyyar at your joke. But did the waatr reach the sakool near the satishun?' Prem Kishan's even louder guffaws at these Punjabi-isms startle the birds in the nearby trees into taking off with loud flaps of their wings.

A beautiful steel-grey Toyota has just sped past us. This is quickly followed by one of the old American Studebakers that one still sometimes sees as families take their evening drives trips on the quiet stretch of Southern Avenue flanking the lakes. It is packed with the members of a large family, obviously off to sample the *phuchka* – Bengali *gol-gappas* – or the fresh-squeezed fruit juices on display in the stalls lining the iron railings along the length of road near us.

'Did you see that beaut, *yaar*?' says Prem Kishan. 'One sexy machine, isn't she? Like that broad's backside over there.'

His colourful vocabulary seems a bit at odds with a classical vocal star in the making, rather more in tune with the pop music crowd. Obviously, like our schoolmates, he is fed on a diet of James Hadley Chase, Harold Robbins, Ellery Queen and other American bestsellers. He could pick up dozens of them from the streetside bookshops lining Gariahat Road just half a kilometer away, I think suddenly, irrelevantly.

Catching myself, I say, 'Toyota and Honda are the up and coming auto brands in Japan. They're swamping the market in the States apparently, even beating out the Volkswagen Beetle and other Jap companies like Datsun.'

'*Arrey yaar*, the States. That's the place to be. Just go for it, my Bong *bondhu*. What'll we ever achieve in this socialist rathole we've created? D'you know they didn't even let the Tatas get into making cars? They could've been making waves with their cars just like the Japs. But not here. We're Indians, *yaar*. Too holy for profit. Even our shit has to be sterile.'

Even as we break into smiles, Nazrul asks him, 'But how would you keep your music up in the States? Yes, there's a cult following there for Ravi Shang-kaar and Ali Ak-baar

Kaan –' humorously pronouncing Ravi Shankar and Ali Akbar Khan the way Americans are wont to. 'You know, The Beatles and Yehudi Menuhin, and all this East-meets-West buzz. But where would you find a serious audience? Or proper students? Or even an atmosphere where you could develop a piece fully? They seem to think that our classical music is some cross between folk music and jazz. Or a way to add ornaments and colour and exciting percussion to modern American music.'

'*Yaar*, I'd worry about that when I get there. It's a land of milk and honey after all,' Prem Kishan drawls. And then, somewhat irrelevantly, he adds, '*Kya smart hote hain ye Umreekan log!*' 'How smart these Americans are!'

'What's that supposed to mean?' Nazrul asks, incredulity dripping from his voice.

'*Yaar*, I'm not a *khaandani* musician like you. My family came as refuges from Lahore, and they brought their love of music with them. Lahore was somewhat like old Delhi in that respect you know, although it didn't have nearly as strong a vocal tradition. But I don't mean to be poor all my life, swallow mounds of dust in the Delhi buses going around teaching music to bored housewives, or some philistine who can't tell the difference between *Bhairavi* and *Marwa*. I want a fancy car, a glamorous wife, all the latest gadgets, *yaar*. The good life.'

'But what does that have to do with Americans being smart?' Nazrul counters.

'*Yaar*, I've seen some of these Yankee visitors to Delhi, you know the hippie types that started flooding in a few years ago,' Prem Kishan replies.

'Yes. The type that take off their slippers and sit on the floor in lotus position even if the room is fully furnished. And listen to your music as though they're about to enter *samadhi* any minute, as if all Indians are in a permanently catatonic or meditative state,' Nazrul says acidly. But this seems lost on our visitor from Delhi.

'*Yaar*, but my family are telling me to go to New York. I've heard that you can get by, giving concerts in Soho in small art galleries and artist's co-ops. And then, gradually build up a fan following, break into the recording circuit, do East-meets-West tracks. It's all red hot there right now. Look at this new album Ravi Shankar's nephew – what's his name – has just brought out. I'd have a car and nice digs in no time *yaar*, before my college mates even make it to UK or the States.'

'Ananda Shankar's the nephew,' Nazrul says as though humouring a child. 'Seems like an interesting fusion – both of musical ideas and sounds – to me, that album of his. Not just any old mish-mash, you know. It's a bit juvenile to think that any old person could do something like that.'

I am fidgeting a bit. I know of Nazrul's general disinterest in such matters, and the conversation seems to be taking an ominous, combative turn. In order to change the subject, I break in, 'I just got a letter saying that I got a two-year fellowship for graduate study at Harvard University in Boston. They forwarded the letter to me from Kanpur. It says it's a very early award, whatever that means.'

'That's great news Aniket,' Nazrul says, jumping up and clapping me on the back. 'On that note, let's have some *chai*.' He motions to the tea-seller a few yards away.

The Whispered Raga

The man approaches and places his large aluminium kettle and small basket with milk and sugar on the ground near us. We ask for three teas.

As he begins pouring out the tea into clay *bhars*, Prem asks, 'Why Kanpur?'

'Oh, I guess you don't know about any of this, Prem,' I say. 'I'm finishing an engineering degree at the IIT there. And the award's in an applied sciences department, so I could switch to something closer to my heart. Engineering leaves me a bit cold – too many black boxes to my taste, too little that's fundamental.'

I can see a smile again on our Delhi visitor's lips. Nazrul is nodding understandingly. 'So what d'you think you'll do?' he asks.

'I'm in two minds. I really want to stay in India, perhaps just join as a research scholar at Calcutta University or the Indian Statistical Institute. Or even IISc, Bangalore or TIFR in Bombay. That way, I can keep up my music. But my *dadu* keeps saying that there are no good jobs after doing pure science.'

'You Bongs are too intellectual for your own good,' our guest chimes in. 'Or maybe just pseudo-intellectual. Why do we need so many scientists and historians and English Lit types in this socialist desert we've built? As it is, all of them either end up abroad or frustrated and suicidal if they stay here. No wonder, seeing how little they're paid.'

I see a look of irritation cross Nazrul's usually smiling countenance. Before he can say anything, I hastily break in, 'My father was from a refugee family too, you know, and made it only because he was lucky enough to get a government scholarship to study medicine. Before he died, he'd talk about how he'd survived during his student years just by drinking water on many days, before the one meal of the day he could afford in the evening. And how the city boys from Calcutta's elite families and schools would snicker at his East Bengal accent and the old hand-me-down guard's overcoat from his elder brother which he would wear during the winter. He didn't want any of us to suffer the way he did during his early years.'

This time it seems that I have broken through. Prem Kishan's bluff, carefree expression grows somewhat graver. 'Yes, I know many such stories among the Punjabi and Sikh refugee families in and around Delhi as well,' he says, his tone matching the intensity of his face. 'But be bold, *yaar*. Take the bull by the horns. Beat a path to the States, the quicker the better. Don't be a timid Bong *babu*,' he adds in a now familiar-sounding refrain. 'But I'd better return to the school. I want to shower and get a sound nap. Sureshwari Devi's put me on notice that I need to get up bright and early tomorrow, so I want to catch some shut-eye now.'

'You'll need it, that's for sure,' says Nazrul, reverting to his usual friendly manner. 'We can tell you the way back to the school. It's just a short walk from here.'

But Prem Kishan says, 'I'll probably just take a taxi. I'm pretty beat. See you back at the school.'

As we watch him throw his clay *bhar* in a nearby dustbin and head down the path, Nazrul says, 'A bit of a specimen, isn't he? And he has the gall to call others philistines! A goat on high heels is what he'd have been called in our school, I bet. But anyway, why disturb myself over him? It takes all sorts, I guess.'

'His bark's probably a bit worse than his bite in some ways. What I mean is that it may really just be the way he puts things,' I offer. 'The bluff, well-meaning, but tactless type. There's a fair number of that variety in Delhi, you know. It was quite a rude shock for me after the courtesy of Lucknow when I first used to go there.'

'I don't know about the well-meaning bit. Brash, more like. Want to take a little walk? I'm tired of sitting here.'

'Yes, let's cross to the other side of the train tracks. In fact, how about getting something at the Chat Ghar in Jodhpur Park?' I say.

We begin circling the lake, heading towards the railway tracks. Nazrul puts his arms over my shoulders, and asks, 'Anyway, what d'you think you'll do then, Aniket? Will you go to the US? And what of you and Lopa?'

'It's really the one thing my *dadu*'s ever really pressurised me about. Somehow he feels convinced that I'll end up frustrated and embittered if I do pure science. I'm pretty confused. It seems like I'm damned, no matter what I do. Going for a "good career" with a "*phoren*" engineering degree would mean giving up both of the things which I really love – pure science and music. Or settle for an Indian Ph.D. and then teach science in some college. And keep up music on the side.'

'Ah, but you can always soar on the wings of music. It's enough. With your talent Aniket, it'll always be enough.'

'I wish I was as sure about that, Nazrul. I wish I had your ascetic, frugal, directed nature. Not to mention your family connections. All of the musical pedigree and contacts. No one ever tells you that you'll starve if you don't make it as a musician. You were hailed as a child prodigy. You've been singing at top conferences since you were ten.'

'That's all true,' says Nazrul quietly. 'I could tell you that you've sung at the same conferences, including with me, these last four years too. But that would miss the real point. What do you really want to do with yourself? You'll need to live with that every waking minute of your life you know. And we're only young once after all. Now's the time to stake your all on the goal, to give it everything you have.'

'YOU don't have to worry about succeeding or making it, Nazrul. You've already made it, you've got your life made for you,' I say, a tad irritated.

'One can always find some excuse, Aniket,' he retorts. 'I could say I'm the first one in my family to attend a convent school, and so the whole world's my oyster. The old system of court patronage my family have thrived on is over. It's easy to say that it's a new world, and that no one wants the old purist classical musicians any more. I can claim I'll need to make too many compromises, play to the gallery. Why isn't it better, more profitable, for me to do something else?'

Seeing me shaking my head, Nazrul adds, 'And what does Lopa say?'

'I wish she'd say something. Anything! She's even paranoid about going out with me ever since Idanbai saw us together at Komala Vilas café.'

'Even though you've been together for so many years now? Since the end of high school!'

I nod. 'Yes. Idanbai's still so afraid that even in this day and age things can't last between us. I'm from a middle-class Hindu family you know, and they're Muslims, and that too from a family of *mirasis*.'

'You don't need to explain all that to me,' Nazrul says. 'All this class structure among musicians really makes me sick. And these awful things my mother and uncles are always saying about the *baijis* and the *mirasis*. D'you know why *sarangi* players really died out?'

'But what's that got to go with anything we're talking about?' I respond, puzzled. 'The harmonium must've put the *sarangi* out of business.'

'No, no, no. No keyboard instrument really picks up the half and quarter notes in our music, or the glissandos, or the *meends* and *shrutis* connecting them. So the *sarangi* really was irreplaceable. It's because the *sarangi* players were all of the *mirasi* caste. They were considered the lowest of the low in the social hierarchy of the music world. Even though they played an incredibly difficult, near-indispensable, instrument. One that was the perfect accompaniment because it could almost mimic anything the human voice can produce. And, unlike other stringed instruments like the *esraj*, retain its sweetness of tone even in the extra-high registers.'

'Idanbai wants Lopa to stay on at the Bhatkhande College in Lucknow after she finishes her degree there' I continue morosely like I didn't register anything Nazrul just said about the sarangi. 'So that we're separated. Now that I'm done at Kanpur, we'd be farther apart than ever.'

'If you go to the US, that'd be taken care of anyway,' Nazrul shrugs.

'Yes. We'd better get going. Let's skip the Chat Ghar for today. Guruji will be upset if we're late for the meeting.' Nazrul agrees, and we turn and begin to retrace our steps.

'Not to mention mother,' Nazrul adds, continuing my train of thought. 'She insists that I do an hour of *chilla* the last few weeks before a big performance. And she'll make you do it as well since this'll be our first joint public concert in some time. As it is, she was strongly opposed to our *jugalbandhi* at an event as big as this one – you know, the school's annual festival.

'Oh I know auntie,' I say with a smile. 'Just the other day she was fuming about these new electronic transducers and mikes. "All this new-fangled gimmickry! What's our music coming to?" she keeps saying. But she sure loves your new *swar-mandal*.'

'Oh, it's something, isn't it?' asks Nazrul, and I nod vigorously in agreement. 'I love the feel of it, the polished frame and the ivory knobs and inlay. And the sound. It's divine! Absolutely ravishing.'

'It's such a complete accompaniment for a vocalist, isn't it?' I say. 'Isn't it surprising that no one thought of something like it before Bare Gulam Ali Khan?'

'Necessity, right? It's always the mother of invention. He needed it to practice through the night at crematoria.

My mother says that he practiced every waking moment, except when he was eating. No wonder, he had such incredible speed and clarity and control.'

And then Nazrul interrupts himself, 'Oh, look! Look! This must be the most beautiful sight in this city, Aniket! Like a *raga mala* in the sky. Like *Raga Puriya* or *Kalyan*. No, no, it's *Marwa*, definitely *Marwa*. The exquisite combination of the *rekhab* and *dhaivat*, the *re* and *la*, it captures just this moment!'

I am accustomed to these poetic outbursts from him. Looking almost imploringly at me, he continues, 'Don't you feel it, Aniket? This agonised, hushed weeping of this twilight hour, like a pining lover, a wail of agony in this city of rich and poor alike. All suffering in some way, seeking who knows what transcendence, some touch of spirit.' He is pointing into the far distance.

Following his finger, I see a large flock of cranes framed on the sides by the black, hulking silhouettes of the Lake, Anderson, and Rowing Club buildings at the water's edge, and by the lengthening shadows and multihued vortices rippling the surface below.

Then, as the gongs of the Buddhist temple peal out again, they speed, like a shower of arrows released in perfect unison by some master archer, into the luminous steel-blue orb limned between darkened Earth and sky by the spreading rays of the now-vanished sun.

1.3

It is celebration time. One of the school's upcoming stars, Rita Mahalanobis, who arrived from Gauhati two years earlier to train under Idanbai, is to be formally inducted as a *ganda-bandh* or official student of Sureshwari Devi. Things have not gone well between her and Idanbai, and Sureshwari has been only too willing to step into the breach.

Today's event has been partly financed by the new corporate sponsor of the school, Messrs Batliwala and Sons, importers of wines, fine spirits, and other sundries. The family of Parsee owners trace their lineage back to Calcutta's earliest horse breeders and are among the three original Indian families allowed membership to the Royal Calcutta Turf Club in the nineteenth century. They have also provided the city with two mayors, several palatial mansions that are rumoured to be among the grandest East of Suez, several watering holes for the city's elite, and numerous charitable institutions and schools.

Whispers of questionable ethics have always dogged them, right from the days of the family patriarch in the 1880s, when the family fortunes were first established by dubious dealings in Burma teak, through the years of wartime profiteering in CP teak, tea, foodstuffs and perishables, and down through the post-Independence days of influence peddling and license-snatching for their newer import and colliery businesses across eastern India.

Their credentials in the world of North Indian classical music are more tenuous, at best of quite recent vintage. Sureshwari Devi has always been of the firm persuasion that these are non-existent. In her regal tone, she regularly registers her protest against the new developments.

In his milder, absent-minded way, Guruji would respond, 'But times are changing, Sureshwari. Where will the support come from? The abolition of the princely kingdoms almost killed the old patronage system for our music, and now doing away with the privy purses of the princely families has put paid to the little that was still left. In this country, where the government of independent India supports such few schools to preserve or promote our music, what other option is there?'

Sureshwari Devi would jerk her head in her imperious manner, evade the question, and, looking in the direction of anyone else that might be present, respond with a verbal fusillade, 'I suppose you're right. Wine bottlers. D'you know the story of the wine merchant listening to the legendary Ustad Natthan Khan in Bombay? The Ustad would send his *shagird*, his disciple, the great Bhaskar Rao Bakhle, to buy his spirits from a liquor store each night. So, one evening, the Parsee storeowner came to see who this daily client was.'

Guruji would look towards us with his usual absent-minded bewilderment, mixed in with the air of a hapless teacher talking to a retarded child, 'I know Sureshwari, I know. On hearing that it was a singer, the wine merchant asked to listen to the Ustad. Who knows what he understood of this *pucca* music, but he left only three rupees as a token of his appreciation.'

Sureshwari Devi would reply, 'Yes, yes. Natthan Khan said, "He could at least have gifted us a bottle. But to each their own level of generosity I suppose. Anyway, these three rupees will cover three days of grocery shopping.'"

Guruji would usually nod, or register his acquiescence in some other way.

Sureshwari would then pounce, 'So you see the sort of philistine into whose hands you're putting us? A glorified seller of spirits! Bhaskar Rao was so outraged, and his devotion to his guru was such that he vowed never to buy liquor from that store again, even if it meant walking miles to go to another store.'

Guruji's regular response would be, 'But even you must realise that those days are gone forever, Sureshwari. What can all that have to do with us today?' He knew, even before he said it, that his words could not fall on deafer ears.

****

In keeping with changing times, today's event is being held at the Calcutta Club. The suggestion for the venue has come from Mr. Cyrus Madan, Managing Director of Batliwala and Sons.

Rita Mahalanobis' family, appropriately enough, is a wealthy distributor of both timber and alcohol throughout Assam and the north-eastern states. Her parents have jumped at this chance to showcase their daughter before the city's elite. As for the rest of the school, everyone is more than a little apprehensive about how this forced marriage of North Indian classical music with the city's cocktail-cum-commercial circuit will fare.

Mr. Madan has just entered the banquet hall where the event is being held. He is assiduously doing the rounds of the room, beaming at someone here, pumping a hand there, or crossing over to greet some particularly powerful or influential figure in the city with arms outstretched and an exclamation or a kiss on the cheek. As he comes closer, I notice that, even by his natty dressing standards, he has really outdone himself today. He seems to have stepped straight out of an advertisement for Zodiac ties.

Guruji has done his bit today, albeit with some misgivings. Among the guests are our neighbours in the plush Wellesley Mansions flat, which, my *Dadu*, a leading lawyer in Lucknow, has gifted to us now that my *didi* – older sister – has moved to Australia for higher studies and that his health does not allow him to keep up his Calcutta practice. The families in the building are all well-heeled, but like most of central Calcutta – the old White Town of colonial days, decidedly westernised. Even an optimistic estimate of our neighbours' combined exposure to North Indian classical music would probably total one complete concert among the entire group.

Now there is a sudden commotion outside. Through the French windows and the open wooden Venetian blinds, I see three of the Club bearers dragging a burly figure out of the back seat of a taxi. It is a ludicrous scene – three grown men in colonial-era bearer's uniforms staggering under the weight of an inebriated figure at least double their size.

As they come closer, Guruji draws a sharp breath. 'Christmas has certainly come early this year,' he says with some embarrassment. 'That's Mr. D'Souza, the first of our esteemed neighbours.'

We leave the lobby area and walk over to the table on the verandah where the Regals, the family who rent the flat above us, are seated. They are talking to Mr. Aratoonian – another neighbour – and a tall man with a military bearing. 'Hullo, Vishnuji,' Mr. Aratoonian says. 'Meet Mr. Chowdry, the GOC in C, Eastern Command. He commands the Fort William garrison. We're golf partners.'

We shake hands. I can see that Guruji is uncomfortable. We are saved by Cyrus Madan who walks up to us with his perennial smile. After introductions are made all around, Madan begins what by now is his familiar spiel, 'I must mention, gentlemen, that Guruji here has done me the great honour of placing the charge of his great music school in our hands. We're certainly happy to support an institution of Indian music. We've been doing it ever since British times for Western classical music – the Calcutta School of Music, you know. But this will be our first effort in Indian music.'

I see Mr. Aratoonian nodding. The General's expression is non-committal. He breaks in, 'This is really all lost on me, I'm afraid. My knowledge of Indian classical music is limited to a few old semi-classical film songs like *Madhuban me Radhika nache re*, you know.'

A bearer passes, and we pause to pick up soft drinks and some of the Club's famed assortment of in-house snacks, including a handful of mushroom triangles and chicken *samosas*. Mr. Aratoonian says, 'I think I need something a bit stronger. Please excuse me for a few minutes.' The General nods in agreement, and we watch the two step back into the lobby and stop at the bar running along the length of the inner wall. The thread of music has been broken.

We talk for some more time about this and that. After Mr. Aratoonian and the General return, Guruji brings up the matter of support for the school. Both his attempts to broach the subject meet with polite nods and promises to explore possible avenues of support. But each time, the conversation seems to gravitate back to other things – the races, the state of the city's clubs, new restaurants that have opened.

A Catholic priest in the familiar robes of the Jesuit fathers of St. Xavier's enters through the front door. Father Mairlot from my school is someone with a real passion for Indian music. He visits us often in our flat, and is here today at Guruji's invitation.

'I really would much rather have come to an actual concert at your school, Vishnu,' he says, waving and walking over to us. 'But I suppose I'll need to make do with a short programme for the *ganda-bandh* ceremony.'

Guruji smiles and appears a bit relieved to see him. 'At least it'll be better than Australia,' he says. 'You'll find no Indian classical music there at all.'

'You're off to Australia then?' the General asks.

'Unfortunately, yes. Much as I love India, I see very little future for myself or our Jesuit Order here, you know. I've spent forty years here. I remember a time when

Calcutta was the second city of the Empire. And so central in the consciousness of the Catholic Church. And now, with all this leftist turbulence, everyone is moving to Delhi and Bombay.'

'I beg to differ with you a bit there Father, if I may,' interjects Mr. Aratoonian.

Another waiter appears with a tray of drinks and snacks. After he leaves, Mr. Regal says, 'We're off to Australia as well. 'My company's moving to Delhi too. And two of my older son's classmates have had their family businesses facing lockouts and strikes on a continuous basis over the last year. So many other firms have folded already. But continue, Phillip,' he tells Mr. Aratoonian. 'Let's hear your angle on this.'

'You know that people said the same during the communal riots of the Partition and Independence days. But things settled back to normal. I still have faith in this country. If you think of the mass ethnic pogroms we Armenians faced in Turkey, I'd still place my bets on this country any day.'

'But not Calcutta. Maybe Delhi and Bombay?' Mr. Regal asks.

'We have priests in our school who'd say the same as Mr. Aratoonian. And who have great sympathy for the Naxalites for instance,' Fr. Mairlot says. 'But with Asian immigration to Australia and Canada being much easier now, we're seeing an ever-larger emigration of our students.'

Out of the corner of my eye, I see Idanbai and Lopa enter the Club. We raise our hands in greeting, as Mr. Madan accosts them and ushers them in our direction. It has taken Guruji considerable effort to convince Idanbai to hand her student over to Sureshwari Devi in this unfamiliar club setting.

The conversation veers around for some time to Fr. Mairlot's new book on the various North Indian *gharanas*, and his quest to interview and record as many of the leading older musicians as possible before their art is forever lost. For once, even the Regals, and Aratoonian and his generalissimo seem genuinely interested. Idanbai walks up to us and another round of introductions are made. But Lopa is nowhere to be seen.

'Let me tell you a fascinating story I heard from the aged Ustad Alladiya Khan a few years ago,' Fr. Mairlot says at one point. 'He told me that the greatest *khayal* singer he ever heard was Bare Mubarak Khan of Atrauli. But another of his ancestors from the same town was Ustad Monotol Khan.'

'My mother once met him,' Idanbai breaks in, smiling. 'He was an ascetic who went around visiting temples or the *dargahs* of *pirs*. He lived in the jungle in the middle of nature.'

'Yes,' Fr. Mairlot says. 'The story I heard was that the local king once asked his courtiers whether there was any musician whose singing brought tears to everyone's eye. And their answer was this same Monotol Khan.'

'So they had him brought to court, I expect,' Mr. Aratoonian says.

'Well, only with the utmost difficulty. By subterfuge actually, the Father says.'

'And?'

'Well, as you can guess, his singing indeed brought tears to every eye, with the king himself sobbing uncontrollably near the end. But the real twist came at the end when the king asked him for any boon that was within his power to grant. And the Ustad replied, "I have only one request your majesty. Please never request me to come to your court again."'

Everyone breaks into chuckles and smiles. Idanbai adds, 'I think he was once waylaid by some dacoits in the Chambal area of central India, near the Rajasthan-MP border. And he even had them eating out of his hands after he sang for them.'

Large containers of food are now brought and placed on the long tables which line three sides of the large back lawn onto which the club's verandah opens. Guruji turns to me and says under his breath, 'I know that Sureshwari likes to make an appearance. But where are they? It's almost time for the food to be served.'

As if on cue, I see the bearer at the entrance raise his hand in a *salaam* as the door swings open to reveal the figure of Sureshwari Devi, resplendent in white chiffon with her trademark diamonds glittering in her ears and nose. Even by her standards, today's is quite an entrance. She has deliberately placed Nazrul, immaculate in a silk *achkan* and *sherwani*, between herself and Rita Mahalanobis. Everyone in the lobby turns to look at them as Rita, clinging to Nazrul's arm, makes a show of removing the small tiara on her head which matches the exquisite silver and *mina* set on her neck and arms.

I can see the surprise on Guruji and Idanbai's faces. It has been no secret in the school that Rita has been assiduously cultivating Sureshwari Devi. She is undoubtedly a gifted singer. Marrying into a family like Sureshwari Devi's is an entirely different proposition though – it would immediately thrust her into the front ranks of the country's upcoming vocalists. Indeed, her ministrations have mellowed the older singer's normal petulance to such a degree that some people in the school have begun referring to them as *saas-bahu*, or mother-in-law and daughter-in-law.

Even so, such a public display is unprecedented. Guruji leans towards me and asks, 'Have they agreed on something, Aniket? This feels almost like an announcement of an engagement.'

'Not that I know of, Guruji. I know that Nazrul has been in two minds on the matter,' I reply. 'And neither he nor Rita is really sure how the Mahalanobis family would react to such an alliance.'

But can this mean that Nazrul has made up his mind? As Guruji nods, I think perhaps he's given in. An otherworldly dreamer like Nazrul. What chance does he have anyway against that gorgon?

During dinner, Rita Mahalanobis' usual solicitous attentions to Sureshwari Devi appear to extend to Nazrul to an unusual degree. Several times, as she goes about arm-in-arm with him, I catch snippets directed at our corporate guests, like, 'Oh, Nazrul is so fantastically gifted. If only he wasn't so shy, he'd take the country by storm.' On the third occasion, I see Nazrul looking haplessly in our direction. He looks resigned, but his face is quite flushed.

About half an hour later, I am standing at the front door with Mr. Madan, seeing off some of the guests. Madan is busy pumping everyone's hands and reminding them of their promises of scouting around for funds to support the school. I excuse myself. Going past the bar, down the corridor leading to the toilet, I hear hushed voices in one of the side rooms. As I walk past, someone whispers emphatically, 'But what're you afraid of? What can go wrong?' I halt, realising I have eavesdropped on Rita and Nazrul.

****

The *ganda-bandha* ceremony rounds out the evening. It has been stripped down to the bare bones. Guruji has devised it keeping both the after-dinner ambience, with the guests nursing drinks on the Club lawns, as well as the relations between Idanbai and Sureshwari Devi in mind.

Rita Mahalanobis places a tray of gifts in front of both women. As her past guru, Idanbai then requests that she sing. The *tanpura* has been kept ready, and the token one line is quickly completed. The affair concludes with Sureshwari Devi gathering Rita to her breast saying, '*Beti*, from today you're mine, my daughter and my student.'

For once, Sureshwari Devi betrays neither triumph nor acerbity. The crowd, unaware of the charged relations between the two prima donnas, applaud the gracious, amicable ways of the music world.

1.4

We have been ushered to the balcony of a large flat in the new multi-storied Apsara II Apartments on Middleton Row. Guruji has brought Nazrul, Prem Kishan and me to see a mystery man from Rajasthan who can apparently read faces. All our protests have been to no avail.

We have chosen to sit outside, the better to sun ourselves in the winter glow. People scurry past the YWCA and bank building on the opposite footpath. Office-goers crowd around hawkers selling hot noontime lunches at the gate. And others emerge from the entrance of the Barrett's furniture store and the Kalimpong Home Products bakery on our side of the street.

The room through which we have entered opens onto the balcony through large French windows. A servant brings us a tray with tea and some mango *sandesh* and *chum-chums*, both traditional Bengali sweets – one, light and crumbly; the other, harder and stuffed. After setting his load down, he says, 'Madam said that the *saab* will come out soon.'

The gentleman who emerges a short time later has a striking appearance. At least six-feet-two in height, his sharp features are mellowed by age to an expression that I can only describe as saintly. Even at this relatively early hour, he is dressed in saffron-hued silk robes, with a matching silk turban wrapped around his head. There are no other signs that often mark a guru or a *baba* – no beard or bead garlands or markings on the forehead. A gentle smile is playing about his lips as he approaches us. We rise from our chairs and he extends his hand to each of us in turn. He makes no verbal response to our greetings, folding his hands in front of his chest in a *namaskar* instead. Then, slipping into one of the chairs, he gestures to us to resume our seats and continue drinking our tea.

As the lady of the house emerges a few minutes later with a slate-board, of the sort young children use in school, the reason for the lack of verbal greeting becomes clear. The guru is deaf and dumb. She greets each of us in turn, and then, turning towards the *baba*, writes on the slate, 'They are friends of mine and would like to ask you some questions.'

His beaming smile leaves no room for doubt about his agreeability. Bending slightly in front of him, and then looking towards us as well, she adds, 'I have to leave for a meeting at the Tolly Club, *baba*. I will be back in two hours, and then we can all have lunch.'

As the *baba* raises his right hand in a gesture of blessing and inclines his head signalling assent, Guruji says, 'No, no, Mrs. Phutnani. We will just spend some time with *Baba* and then take our leave. Thank you for the offer, but please don't trouble yourself with arranging for lunch. We really should go after that. There're things to do at the school.'

After she has taken her leave, *baba* picks up a *chum-chum* from the tray and follows it up with a glass of water. Then, picking up the slate, he writes, 'I will tell you each something. After that, if you have additional questions, you can ask me?'

We nod and smile. He then turns in my direction and stares intently at my face. Just as I am beginning to wonder how long the examination will last, he scribbles, '*Larta tej, parta tej, layakata tej*' or 'Fights hard, studies hard, has strong potential.'

Nazrul says with a smile, 'The first two certainly apply, don't they, Aniket?'

I nod but think it's quite a general statement that could apply to lots of people.

Baba continues to stare at me. He erases the slate and writes, '*Shani* (Saturn) will impede you for the next twenty years. You have just come under its *dasha*.' As I am wondering what to make of this piece of mumbo-jumbo, he adds, 'It will hurt your career, but most of all, it will be an insurmountable barrier to marriage. But eventually, you'll taste all the pleasures of Earth.'

I'm convinced by now that the *baba* makes educated guesses based on his subject's appearance and manner, and perhaps any other verbal leads that might be provided to him. I certainly know nothing whatsoever about *Shani* or its *dasha*, whatever that might mean. As to my marital affairs, it is probably pure guesswork or a random comment. 'Perhaps that's what it is,' I decide, smiling inwardly. 'Say something that sounds impressive. Or scary. I bet he'll ask for money next to propitiate *Shani*. Or to taste the pleasures of Earth.'

Nazrul looks a bit perplexed, and a broad smile wreathes Prem Kishan's features. Guruji seems lost in thought.

Baba, however, is in no mood to grant me easy satisfaction. After about a minute, he wipes the slate clean again and writes, 'You are fated to settle abroad. But the major part of your success will be achieved in India. Do you have any questions?'

By now, I am out of my depth. If he is indeed the typical trickster of the kind one sees at every major street crossing in Calcutta, not to mention in the advertisements festooning the pavements and the newspapers, he is certainly quite a suave, polished customer. I shake my head indicating the negative. No need for any more of this bunkum.

The *baba* looks at me for a second, and then makes as if to open his mouth. But he checks himself and shakes his head sideways, clucking his tongue loudly, rather like a chicken.

Turning abruptly to the smiling Prem Kishan, seated next to me, he says, '*Hoshiar beta. Tum bahut chaalaak ho. Lekin eisa asar na ho ki tum zameen aur asmaan ke beech latak jao.*' 'Careful son. You're very smart. But make sure that you don't end up suspended between heaven and earth.'

This time, we are all a bit rattled. The smile disappears from Prem Kishan's face. 'What does that mean, Baba?' he asks. Baba gestures towards his left ear, shaking his head to indicate his deafness, and holding out the slate and chalk. Prem Kishan takes them and repeats his question in writing.

Baba shrugs his shoulders. Then, taking back the slate, he writes, 'It is hard to be specific. But I foresee danger, and eventually an uncomfortable situation arising from your smartness.'

Prem Kishan doesn't react to this. The *baba* seems to temporarily have pricked the balloon of effusiveness that usually surrounds him like a halo. He's trying to scare Prem, I assume. The money bit comes next, doesn't it?

Once again, I am denied satisfaction by the *baba*. Turning next to Nazrul, he says, '*Tumhe kuch dukh jhelna parega, beta. Lekin tum mamooli insaan nahi ho. Tum pir banoge. Sur ke saagar me doob jaoge. Isi zamin par tum aasmaan pe raaz karoge.*' 'You will have to surmount some setbacks and sadness, son. But you're no ordinary person. You'll be a *pir*. You'll become immersed in an ocean of music. You'll reside in Heaven on this Earth.'

'What kind of setbacks, *Baba*?' Nazrul asks.

'Go to the *Poush Mela* in Shantiniketan this month as you're planning,' is his cryptic, startling reply. 'You'll begin to find the man of your heart there.'

The rest of the session continues in similar fashion. Nazrul asks some other questions, and then the *baba* speaks to Guruji. I begin to ponder the *baba's* words to the three of us.

They have been quite distinct in all three cases. And also fairly specific. With no mention of money at any point. Is this *baba* a mere charlatan? Or a very sophisticated, confidence-trickster who only comes around to money later, after his clients have been bamboozled and their appetites sufficiently whetted?

I come out of my reverie with a start some time later. Nazrul is shaking me by the shoulder. 'Come on, Aniket. It's time to go.'

As we are taking the lift down to the ground floor where our car is parked, Guruji asks us, 'So what did you make of him?'

'I guess he knew that we were musicians. So his comments about me are easily explained,' Nazrul is quick to say. 'And of course such people always say pleasant things so that you keep coming back.'

'But he didn't say pleasant things to Prem Kishan, did he?' Guruji says with a smile.

'He was just spouting pleasant-sounding things, Aniket on Earth, me between Heaven and Earth, and Nazrul in Heaven. Sounds totally fake to me. Rehearsed lines,' says Prem Kishan. He seems to be trying to laugh it off, but is fooling no one.

'It reminds me of a story regarding *babas* of this kind,' I say. 'Two friends, one of whom is concerned about failing his exam, go to a new *sadhu* who has appeared in town. His name is Swami Chapetananda, or the "bliss of slapping", and he sits beneath a tree on the river bank. Rumour has it that anyone administered a whack by the blissful one's holy palm would gain their heart's desire.'

As others laugh, Nazrul says, 'I think I remember reading this one. It's one of Shorodindu Banerjee's Napla, or Napoleon, episodes, right? But I've forgotten the details.'

I nod, and say, 'So Napla and his friend go to the Swami and, sure enough, he lands a real hard slap on Napla's cheek. The sheer force of it makes Napla see stars, and is enough to make the friend think better of undergoing the same experience. But Napla's brains are so addled by the slap that he fails his exam. And then he becomes the laughing stock of the school when the story of how he was slapped gets around.'

'Oh, I remember now!' Nazrul says. 'Napla also fails the exam of the teacher whom he had humiliated and who was out to get him, right?' As I nod, he continues, 'So Napla borrows a friend's pet monkey and takes him to the *sadhu* covered in a sheet, pretending that it's a sick child. And the *sadhu*'s disciples dutifully have a slap administered to the covered figure by their master.'

'And I bet all hell breaks loose,' Prem Kishan guffaws.

'Oh yes, the enraged monkey climbs onto Baba Chapetananda, and pummels him black and blue until he jumps into the river and swims to the far shore, never to show his face again.'

After the laughter dies down, Guruji says, 'But you still didn't answer my question. This *baba* didn't just say pleasant things, nor did he ask for money.'

'I guess we'll have to wait and see,' Prem Kishan says dismissively. 'These charlatans come in many guises, especially in this land of so-called holy men, and many gullible, superstitious people. The best we can do is to give him the benefit of the doubt.'

'Now, waiting and seeing reminds me of another story,' Nazrul says. 'A grandfather and his grandson go to an astrologer. After the usual pleasantries, the astrologer does a reading and tells them "I see only one danger for each of you. For you, the grandfather, the danger will come from a blow to the head, maybe from a falling brick. And for you, the grandson, it will be from a lion.'

'And?' Guruji asks.

'Well, the grandfather takes to sleeping outdoors, on the terrace. And the grandson takes to systematically destroying any picture or model of a lion that he comes across. And then, at a fair, the grandson scratches himself with a nail that holds together two halves of a wooden lion. And dies of tetanus. And an eagle drops something on the sleeping grandfather's head, and he dies as well.'

'When he is asked, the astrologer then says, "I told you so", right?' Guruji says. 'Well, you are all young – this is the age for revolt and rationalism. I must say that I was struck by this *baba's* unusually strong aura, though. But you'll probably claim that that's all superstitious nonsense.'

As we hail a passing taxi to go back to the school, Nazrul tells Guruji, 'Aniket and I want to visit the musical instrument stores in Chetla. Would you like to come along?'

'I think I'll rest a bit, *beta* and then I have students. But why don't you go with them, Prem?' Guruji suggests. 'It's a nice area to browse around. They sell antique musical instruments too, and you see the craftsmen at work as well. It's such a bright, sparkling day.'

Prem Kishan agrees and I say to him, 'I need to have my *tanpura* repaired, Prem. It's old, my father's. And Nazrul needs some knobs on his swar-mandal tightened.'

'You should also take him to College Street one day,' Guruji adds. 'They have some real treasures by way of music books there, although not as many as in my youth.'

1.5

It is the evening of the first day of Sursagar School's annual music conference. The afternoon has featured an instrumental *jugalbandhi* of sitar and sarod in the style made popular by Pandit Ravi Shankar and Ustad Ali Akbar Khan. That has been followed by a vocal recital by an upcoming male singer from Indore. Both have been technically competent. But neither has made a strong impact on either the audience or the *ustads* among the listeners.

The talk among the guests before the show begins is largely centred on the fireworks that inaugurated last year's festival. Within moments, the curtain rises and I feel a tight knot in my throat as I watch Lopa advance to the centre of the stage. And then some relief as Idanbai emerges from the wings a few moments later. I lean over to Nazrul and Prem Kishan and whisper, 'Thank God Idanbai's there. It might be hard for Lopa alone to create an impression.'

'Yes, Idanbai always connects immediately with any audience,' Nazrul whispers back to me.

I nod, and reply, 'But I think Lopa may surprise us though. Today's her big chance, and Guruji's been talking about how far she's come these past few months under her mother's guidance. He says she's outgrown the training stage already, and is sprouting wings.'

'Yes, Guruji's also told me that she's ready to soar, that all the parts of her training have suddenly begun coming together, like a sudden maturing,' Nazrul responds. 'It's rather early for that though.'

Prem Kishan grins, 'I've heard of Idanbai since I was this high,' and he places his hand against his leg, below the knee. At that height, he must have been a toddler. 'And of course, on radio and LPs. But today'll be the first full-length concert I'll get to see.'

'You're in for a treat,' the lady over on the other side of him says with a smile.

Turning to her, and then back to us, Prem Kishan replies, 'I'm certainly hoping so. But I keep hearing within our *gharana* that the Kirana people are lax with their development of *bol-baat* and even the rhythmic parts, the *layakari*. It's really hard to judge in a twenty-minute radio programme, or even on an LP, you know.'

Somewhat unusually, four *tanpura*s have been brought on stage. One is in Lopa's hands, and she and three of Idanbai's other students are twisting the knobs and strumming the strings in a dissonant cacophony that soon settles into a more agreeable resonance as the instruments fall into tune.

The master of ceremonies gestures questioningly towards the artistes onstage and, seeing their nods of assent, does the introductions. Rather surprisingly, Idanbai will sing first, followed by Lopa.

Idanbai is already cocking her head sideways, closing her eyes and raising her left hand next to her face preparing to start. We are settling into our chairs, waiting for the first note to emerge, when she suddenly pricks up her ears and pauses. Turning back to the person holding the third *tanpura*, she gestures for it to be handed to her. As this is done, in one swift motion, she unerringly twists one of the tuning knobs, then strums the corresponding string, and, nodding to herself, returns it to the player.

'Whew,' I say, as applause ripples through the hall.

'See what I mean, Prem?' Nazrul says. 'She picked out which one of the sixteen strings behind her back was slightly off-key just by ear. Quite something, even for her.'

As Idanbai settles back into her former pose and raises her left hand once again, there is a commotion outside. The heavy curtain over the *pandal* door is drawn back and Sureshwari Devi makes her usual regal appearance. As she noisily picks her way through the aisles and then wends her way into the second row of listeners, Idanbai's hand settles back on her lap even as her look of concentration changes to a studied impassivity. Sureshwari Devi is intentionally taking her time and being as noisy as possible, rustling the folds of her *Banarasi* silk *sari*, clanking her heavy gold bangles and pausing every few minutes to wipe her brow daintily with her handkerchief or to smile and wave to various people in the audience.

When she finally settles into her seat, Nazrul hisses into my ear, 'I wish she'd stop this. She really has her knife into Idanbai. It makes me want to melt into the earth with shame.'

'But what's the reason behind it?' Prem Kishan asks.

'It's a long story. And I don't know the half of it. She just can't get over it. Even last night, when I was telling her a bedtime story, she kept muttering, "That *khunsat dain*, the nosy witch. I'll show her tomorrow. A *baiji* share the same stage with me." I've given up on telling her anything about it though.'

'You have to tell her stories like a little child!' Prem Kishan says.

'Yes, and they have to have a happy ending. Otherwise, she throws a fit. Almost becomes hysterical, and won't sleep all night. You know, once my story didn't have a happy end....'

He is interrupted by an abrupt 'Shh' from a woman in the row behind us. I notice Guruji glowering at us. And Idanbai, seated just a few feet away on the raised stage, has also craned her neck to look for the source of the chatter among the audience. We shush ourselves.

The silenced *tanpura*s strike up again. With the first lines, plucked as though they were out of thin air, Idanbai seems already in some state of supplication. She proceeds to develop the raga *vistaar* of the slow *khayal* in the lyrical, romantic style pioneered by Ustad Abdul Karim Khan. Avoiding the rhythmic development of the *bandish* and *bahalwa* of *bara khayals,* she goes on to her usual *bol-taans* in today's *chota khayal.*

Prem Kishan shakes his head a bit perplexedly, perhaps at the lack of the pounding *layakari* characteristic of his Agra school. But, as Idanbai launches into *taans* woven through with rapid *sapat taans* like rapier-thrusts, the audience seems to awake from its hypnotised stupor, and the smile returns to our Delhi friend's face.

Nazrul looks questioningly across Prem Kishan at me. I can almost read his mind from the way his face is contorted, 'Where're those beautiful *Kirana sargams?*' These melodic permutations of sung notes were introduced by Ustad Abdul Karim Khan, adapted from the south Indian or Carnatic style, but with much less use of *gamaks*. As Idanbai brings the piece to a rousing crescendo, it becomes clear that she has decided to forsake them today.

'Where're the *sargams?*' someone in the knowledgeable Calcutta audience calls out. Idanbai smiles and inclines her head slightly in acknowledgment. Her reasons became clear as she launches into Ustad Abdul Karim Khan's immortal *thumri Piya Bin Nahi Aawat Chain*. As she now interlaces its delicate *sargams* into exquisite lines, rending each into the air with delicate twirls and arabesques of her left wrist each time, they seem like gossamer threads weaving some magic carpet.

'They have the same effect as Alladiya Khan's exquisite *taans*,' Nazrul whispers.

'Only built up even more delicately,' I say. 'No *palta* or rapid *mirkhandi sargam* could match the effect of this.'

'Yes, she's always had exquisite taste and sense of measure.'

And now she returns to the refrain, phrasing and drawing it out a shade differently each time. The technical perfection of the earlier piece has given way to Idanbai's natural warmth and passion in this lighter, more expressive song. She isn't called the queen of *thumri* for no reason.

As the marvellous interplay of the beat and her shifts in emphasis, and the wordplay embedded in the magic of the legendary musical enunciation or *sur lagana* immortalised by Ustad Abdul Karim Khan begin to sink in, I feel as though I have become the desolate, pining lover of whom she sings. That she is wringing out every last bit of emotion from my heart. The tears that have begun to sting every eye in the hushed marquee tells me I am not alone in feeling this. Idanbai's own face has grown flushed and her eyes red. And the light glints off wet eyelashes onstage as well.

****

We are back in our seats after a short break. 'Why d'you think she chose to sing before Lopa?' Nazrul asks, leaning towards me.

I shrug. 'I'm sure that she has a good reason. Maybe, that's the reason for all the secrecy during Lopa's *riyaz* these last few months. And Guruji's comments about her.'

'Idanbai will be a hard act to follow though,' Prem Kishan says. We nod in agreement.

The *tanpuras* have been re-tuned. As Lopa begins, Prem Kishan sits up with a start at the sound of her clear, bell-like voice. The sweet, patient development and intricate *swar vistar* of the Kirana style which follow gradually begin to weave their hypnotic web of intensity and high seriousness. She sings as though she is peeling the layers of an onion note by note in establishing the mood and tone through the *alaap* at a somewhat faster pace than Idanbai did.

Like her mother, Lopa seems to be in some private reverie of her own. She is using notes, the *sargam*, slightly differently from the *mirkhand* style in her exposition. Like Abdul Karim Khansahib himself, the *alaap* seems almost intoxicatingly melodious.

So far, it has been a flawless exposition of *gharana* singing, startlingly perfect for a twenty-two-year-old, even one who had been hailed as a prodigy since the age of six. Just as we have begun to sink deeper into the mellifluous river of melody that is pouring out, she accelerates and launches into her first *taan*. There is an immediate cry of '*Hai, hai!*' from one of the *ustads* seated in the first row.

But what is this! So far, the *taans* in all the music that I have ever heard – whether of the Agra, Gwalior, Jaipur, Patiala Sahaswan or any other *gharana* – have followed a pattern. Once one has heard a few of them, the pattern of the rest is essentially predictable. But this is the first time I am hearing *taans* and *sargam* that are all over the vocal spectrum. They swoop upwards to the ultra-high octave before diving swiftly down to the lowest one, and then do something entirely different the next time around. No pattern is discernible at all. And yet, the overall effect is one both of startling power and novelty. The harmonium player, unable to keep up, throws up his hands in despair and gestures heavenwards.

Next, Lopa begins effortlessly mixing in *gamaks* even into the *duni* and *chouduni* – or double – and quadruple-speed, *taans*, almost like actual lightning flashes frissoning the air as they scorch our bodies. Even at the highest speeds, there isn't the slightest loss of clarity and resonance, or the *daana* of the notes, nor any gesticulations or sign of strain in her face or body. As she returns to the refrain, the *phirats* (the return flourishes) display the same startling variety and unpredictability.

There are already rolls of applause in the background. And then, as Lopa brings the piece to a rousing climax, Guruji rises to his feet. The next instant the first few rows where the *ustads* and the cognoscenti of the city's musical circles sit have come alive with a thunderous chorus of *'Hai, hai!'*, *'Kya baat, kya baat!'* and *'Wahs'*.

I know that we have just witnessed history being made. So this has indeed been the reason for all the secrecy, as well as Guruji's comments, about Lopa's *riyaz* these last few months.

Lopa is on her feet now, acknowledging the applause by joining her hands in a *namaste*, alternated with a courtesied gesture of *adaab* in front of her face in the Muslim manner. Idanbai, standing and beaming beside her daughter, has been the architect of this resounding success, with Guruji a willing helper.

'As usual, Idanbai's gauged the impact to perfection,' Nazrul almost yells out to us over the cacophony of applause and cries of appreciation. 'Hats off to her!'

And by letting Lopa perform after her, she is signalling Lopa's coming of age. And maybe even the gradual passing of the torch to her.

1.6

I am alone in one of the school's rehearsal rooms strumming listlessly on a *tanpura*. It is raining outside and, from the window, I can see people near the Lansdowne Road-Southern Avenue crossing already wading through ankle-deep water.

The conference participants have been taken for an excursion to Belur and Dakshineshwar today. But I have stayed back, feigning tiredness.

I have no desire to practice, or to do anything at all for that matter. I feel sick at heart.

Lopa's singing two nights ago seems to have accentuated the trouble in our relations even more in my mind. I seem to alternate between a feeling of acute pain coursing down my right side and complete numbness.

I scratch the surface of the *tanpura* almost instinctively, kneading and worrying away at a groove where the mother-of-pearl inlay meets the wood. There is a clap of thunder, the lights flicker and then become steady again. The stationary goods store across the road has been plunged into darkness.

I rise to place a record on the turntable of Guruji's ancient gramophone. There is a stack of 78 rpm discs, but I am in no mood to listen to some old classical master. I look across the room to where Guruji's spool tape recorder lies. 'Spools have better quality of recording', he always insists, as though trying to reassure himself. I pick out a spool containing the songs of the old Bengali film *Monihaar* from the ones lying there, insert it into the sprockets, tighten the loose segment of tape, and begin playing.

Just as Hemanta Mukherjee's lilting *Keno gelo porobash-e bolo bodhu-aa* (*Why did my lover flee abroad*) begins, I hear a rattle. I assume it is from something outside. But a few minutes later, there is a loud knocking downstairs. It is Lopa. She is drenched from the knees downwards, but has had the presence of mind to grab a *bhar*, the roadside clay cup of tea from the stall across the street before entering.

I am a bit startled. I haven't seen her for weeks, ever since Idanbai saw us together and expressed her displeasure. 'Hi Aniket,' she says with a quick smile. 'I've come to see you.'

'How did you know I'd be here?'

'Oh, Guruji told me," she says offhandedly as she places the tea on the floor, next to my *tanpura*. 'He said we could talk here in private. He'll be here in about an hour's time.'

'Oh Lopa!' I say. 'Thank you, thank you, thank you!' The world suddenly seems a much brighter place. All the heartache and anguish of the past weeks seems gone. I reach out for her and we embrace. I hold her against my body long and tight. She makes no attempt to break free.

1.7

We hear a key in the lock downstairs and then Guruji's firm tread on the stairs.

After he comes up, we call Lalit the bearer and order some more tea. 'You have class today, don't you Guruji?' Lopa asks him.

Guruji grunts in the affirmative, and then, as Lalit deposits the tray with the tea and snacks, he adds, 'But I want to tell you a story. Both of you.'

'What story, Guruji?' I ask.

'A short one, *beta*. But I want both of you to hear it together. What I want to tell you has to do with your current problems,' he adds, noticing our puzzled faces.

'And you want to tell us a story about this?' I say in what I hope is not a sarcastic tone.

Guruji smiles, and then, turning to Lopa, says, 'Do you know who gave you the name Lopa?'

Lopa shakes her head.

'I suggested two possible names to your mother when she asked me for old Vedic ones to go with Nazneen,' he explains. 'I knew that your mother wanted to signify the nature of Indian music, its origins in both the Hindu and Muslim cultures and traditions of our country. So I suggested either Maitreyi or Lopamudra, both Vedic women of remarkable breadth of learning and wisdom.'

'And Idanbai chose Lopa?' I ask. Guruji nods.

There is an abrupt crackling and rasping in the background followed by the sound of rapid unspooling. The tape has been running all this while and has just reached its end.

'Thank you, Guruji,' Lopa says. 'Thanks for telling me that. But what does this have to do with our problems?'

'You see this young man here?' Guruji smiles. 'His grandfather didn't name him Aniket – for the legendary quester and wanderer of the Upanishads – for nothing, you know. And quite appropriately too. I see many shades of his grandfather in Aniket. The same freethinking. The wanderlust. And also, unfortunately, the same stubbornness.'

'What do you mean, Guruji? This seems like a riddle.' Lopa says after a moment's pause.

'You are both going to face a time of trial, I fear. Maybe even for an extended period. But remember your namesake always. Remember that Lopa's great task was to domesticate her husband, the sage Agastya.'

'But she doesn't want to go forward, even a step!' I say. 'Well, not until today that is,' I add hurriedly as Lopa blushes.

'And that is the other half of the story, my children,' Guruji says. 'Remember that Ghosha, another Vedic heroine, suffered from an incurable disease which kept her a spinster for many years. And it was only after many austerities and efforts that she was cured and could experience wedded bliss.'

'And you think that may be my fate as well?' Lopa asks, the curiosity of a cat writ all over her delicate features.

'That is not for me to say, my child. I'm no astrologer like Nazrul's deaf and dumb face-reader from Rajasthan. But I really am afraid that you may both be in for a real trial by fire.'

Lopa and I stare at him silently, and then at each other.

1.8

It is now the third day of the conference. Another break in the proceedings. Sureshwari Devi is conversing with a foppishly dressed middle-aged man in a suit and tie at the door of the multihued marquee. She is gesticulating agitatedly.

'That's Mr. Bokhari, the new Director of All India Radio Calcutta,' Guruji whispers in my direction. 'He's reputed to be the best-dressed man in the British Commonwealth after Sean Connery. A *pukka* sahib, a chip off the old block.'

'His brother also works for AIR, so they've nicknamed it the BBC, the Bokhari Brothers Corporation,' Nazrul sniggers. 'I bet my mother's arguing with him about the new order he's passed cutting the airtime for classical music to almost half of what it now is.'

As Sureshwari Devi makes off shaking her head, Hyder Khan, the reputed *tabla* player, makes a beeline for the *sahib*.

Soon afterwards, Mr. Madan makes an entrance from the opposite end of the marquee. His eyes fall upon the suited *sahib*. As he approaches him, the *sahib* spins rapidly on his immaculate heels and beats a hasty retreat.

A crestfallen Mr. Madan, spying us, strides up to us instead. 'I thought I'd work on Bokhari a bit,' he sighs. 'The man could bring us some custom, not to mention programmes and recordings.'

'Don't you ever think of anything else?' Nazrul says, the disdain in his voice rather obvious.

'I need to keep things running, Nazrul. Uneasy lies the head that wears the crown, you know.' Madan dishes out maxims like an old man would sweets to his grandchildren.

'D'you know how crowned heads treated music and musicians in days gone by?' Nazrul says. 'Anyway, I'll leave you to your regal woes. I have something urgent to attend to.'

Seeing Mr. Madan's discomfiture, Guruji says, 'Let me tell you some stories about the court of the Maharaja of Jodhpur. In those days, there would be large musical *mehfils* or soirees to mark the birthdays of members of the royal family.'

Idanbai, who has just joined our group, chips in, 'There was a definite caste and class system among the musicians, though. The *tawaifs* sang first to set the stage, and were followed by the *sitar*, *rabab* and *sur-singar* players. And the vocalists, the *dhrupad* and *khayal* singers, performed last of all as they were highest in the pecking order.'

'Actually there were people even lower down the order – the *dhadis* who sang paeans to their patrons,' Guruji says. 'And the muslim *tabla* and *sarangi* players either came from this class or a rung lower, the *mirasis*, who also did the manual labour during the celebrations. It was a feudal setup.'

'But tell me the story of the actual celebrations,' Madan cuts in with his usual joviality. 'Those royal bounders. Feudal is a good word for them. I like it. I really like it. I wish I had their kind of money. I wouldn't need to scrape and scrounge either if I did, you know.'

Guruji smiles and says, 'Well, one story goes that the noblemen were sitting to one side at a *mehfil*. With their bags of money beside them, as was the custom. Ustad Nasir Khan was singing at the palace of the King of Jodhpur's brother Kishori Singhji. And he began the refrain, "*Motiyan meha barase*" or "the pearls rain down."'

'And Kishori Singhji immediately ordered a *tashtari* of pearls to be brought and he began showering them on the carpet at regular intervals with cries of "*Kya baat, kya baat! Subhanallah subhanallah!*"' Idanbai adds, smiling.

'Sure sounds like my kind of *mehfil*,' Madan says wistfully, as usual missing Nazrul's dry smile and wink in my direction.

'On one occasion, Kishori Singhji was so extravagant that he showered three lakh rupees from the royal treasury meant for the troops' salaries on the court's wrestlers and musicians. And then took to his bed on the first of the month when the troops' wages fell due,' says Guruji, laughing.

'He sure was an irresponsible bounder, wasn't he?' I say, turning to Mr. Madan. But he doesn't rise to the bait.

'He then confessed to his brother, and was pardoned for his extravagance,' Guruji continues. He reaches for the *pik-daan* and empties the spittle from his mouth into it. As Mr. Madan grimaces disgustedly, Idanbai walks over to the far corner and grabs a *paan* from the *paan-daan* which is permanently placed there.

'I know you're going to say that you wish you had a big brother Mr. Madan,' Idanbai says with a rare display of humour as she returns. 'Let me tell you a story I heard from my mother.'

'Yes,' Madan sighs, 'I really wish I had lived in times like those.'

'Once, being very pleased with their *dhrupad* singing, the king of Datiya invited the father and son duo of Shaadi Khan and Murad Khan to his court.'

'He was man of considerable musical skill himself. And a true connoisseur,' I add by way of explanation. 'The sort of listener that has all but disappeared in today's crowds of middle-class and nouveau-riche. Not here for the experience, but really for the music.'

'Next you're all going to blame me, and say,"Just like the corporations sponsoring music schools and festivals for the advertisement revenue, replacing patrons who loved the art,"' says Mr. Madan.

'Yes, exactly,' I say.

'Anyway, a silk-covered platform covered with one and a quarter lakhs of silver rupees was built for them,' Idanbai continues. 'And, at the end of the evening's proceedings, the king gifted the *ustads* an elephant laden with all of the silver coins saying, "Khan *sahib*, you should know that you have never seen, nor will you ever see, such a generous king."'

Madan's mouth has fallen slightly open. For all his touted pedigree as a patron of music, the excesses of the old Indian nobility are clearly not an area with which he is familiar. 'And what did the ustad say?' he asks eagerly.

'Actually,' Idanbai says, 'the story goes that he didn't say anything. But, on the way to his hotel in Datiya, he opened the purses and rained the silver coins onto the road. Hearing the clamour from far and near, the king sent messengers to enquire what the matter was.'

'And?'

'The ustad sent back the reply, "It is true that I have never seen as generous a king as you. But you will also not find as large-hearted an ustad as me."'

'I really must tell this story at my next Board Meeting,' Madan says. 'It's unbelievable!'

'But that's not all, Mr. Madan. The King was pleased and sent him back an extra *baksheesh*,' says Idanbai, amused by Madan's childlike fascination with the tale.

'How incredible! How absolutely fantastic! Why can't we have that sort of thing today?' he cries.

'The finer, but feudal traditions give way to modernity, even if that means crass commercialism. That's progress for you. Or dialectics, as all these young Calcutta revolutionaries never tire of reminding us,' Guruji says as he shakes his head with a sad smile.

1.9

Guruji is on stage. The heavy curtains over the entrance to the marquee have been drawn shut, drowning out the sounds of the vendors selling cut fruit, *pani-puri* and soft drinks outside.

And now his guru, Ustad Masit Khan of Bombay, is being helped onto the stage. At 105, he is the senior most surviving member of the Gwalior *gharana*. His performance will be a unique feature of the festival this year.

Alauddin Khan, Badal Khan, Krishnarao Shankar Pandit, Alladiya Khan, and many others survived well into their nineties. But this frail figure – bent forward like a bow with his upper body touching his knees – we wonder whether he will survive this ordeal.

His flowing beard that spreads out on the floor, framed by a pair of upright *tanpura*s – in the hands of Guruji and another of the old ustad's disciples sitting behind him – seems a scene straight out of some magical fable, as though he might be lifted up by the next twanging refrain and spirited off to some land of fairies and elves. Or perhaps he will just vanish as the *tabalchi* waves his nimble fingers over his drums to sound the first resonant *bol*.

The audience gradually falls into a hushed, expectant silence. Now only the *tanpuras* drone on, alone with no companions. Then, as the restive rustlings and coughs and whispers resume, slowly and ever so softly, the sound of a *shadaja*, the tonic note, fills the hall. It travels as though wafting in from afar, approaching us in small, measured steps, coming closer, ever closer. The Ustad's head rises in tandem, filling the sound with his being. In the full minute he takes to straighten, there is no break in the tonic. It grows deeper and deeper and resonates through the hall. How does such resonance emanate from such a broken, run-down frame?

He begins the *alaap*. Forty-five minutes later, his *dhuran-muran, mirs* and *gamaks* have rivalled any singer in his prime. Now sitting upright, our attention knits our brows.

Then he launches into the *chota khayal* or the first piece without showing the percussionist the *sam* or tonic. The *tabalchi*, renowned for his sensitive, intricate accompaniment, begins with *chou-taal*. He plays a few measures, searching in vain for the *sam*. By now we are at the edge of our seats. The Ustad is clearly enjoying this cat and mouse game with the percussionist.

The Ustad calls out over his shoulder to Guruji, loud enough for us to hear from our ringside seats, 'Vishnu Joshi!'

'Yes Ustad,' Guruji says.

'Who's on the *tabla*?' he snorts. Perhaps he doesn't see very well, or just finds it hard to remember names.

'Prasanna Sinha, Ustad,' Guruji says.

'So why doesn't he meet me at the right place? Doesn't he know the beat?' the Ustad says, a mischievous smile deepening the wrinkles round his eyes and lips.

Guruji attempts to track the beat with his hands, but even he, master of *taal* as he is, has trouble doing so. Only the harmonium player seems unperturbed.

And then, perhaps to stir up things even more, the Ustad launches into an unexpected string of *vakra* and *kut*, circuitous, *taans* – with intricate *chut* ornaments lacing the zigzagging strings of notes like sparks threading a flash of lightning. The harmonium player now squints at his instrument, shaking his head and lifting his fingers from the keys as he trails off the notes every now and then. We feel the intricacy of the *sargam* or note combinations immediately, but to follow them note for note would take weeks of repeated listening.

As he returns to the peculiarly cadenced *asthayi* or composition, the Ustad seems to revel in continuously altering the stress at unexpected places. It is a masterly exposition. Finally, the *tabalchi* joins his palms in supplication. Looking at us, and then back at the Ustad, he says, '*Huzoor*, you're my senior by far. I'm like your child. Please take me along with you.'

'*Kya*, you've already lost your *prasannata*, your joy!' the Ustad jokes, playing on the meaning of the accompanist's name.

We are thoroughly enjoying the proceedings. 'He's so incorrigibly mischievous at this age,' Nazrul whispers in my ear. 'Imagine what he must have been like when he was younger!'

What happens next takes us by surprise. At the play of words on his name, the *tabalchi* seems to stiffen. He is famous in his own right after all, his posture seems to indicate. 'Just a moment, Ustadji,' he says, turning in our direction. Before our astonished gazes, he whips out a candle and a lighter. 'You are my honoured senior, Ustad,' he says, lighting the candle with a ceremonial flourish. 'In our tabla *gharana*, we say that a *mehfil* never really warms up if the *taans* don't last the length of a burning candle.'

The challenge is clear. The Ustad laughs and says, 'As long as your *theka* lasts, my *tarana* will continue.' As they begin again, Nazrul whispers to me, 'This is taking a dangerous turn.' Yes indeed. My throat suddenly begins to feel dry.

For the next fifteen minutes, as the Ustad sings *tora* after rapid *tora*, the *tablachi* accelerates to ever faster cycles of his *na-dhin-dhin-na bol*s while his *bnaya*, bass drum on his left, provides a slower, hypnotic counterpoint. The hall is afire.

As the Ustad commences his *tarana*, the *tablachi* launches into his *lahara* or *upaja*, the seemingly endless string of *bols* resounding like gunshots off the *tabla* as his fingers disappear into a blur of whirring skin and bone. The Ustad yells out, '*Theka*!' He has returned to half-speed and is revelling in the beat now, tasting the *mazaa* as we are wont to call it. Prasanna Sinha slows down to match the tempo.

The Ustad yells out again, '*Theka*!' He seems to be tiring and is asking to return to a slower beat. But some demon seems to have taken hold of the *tabalchi*. He appears oblivious of his surroundings and of the Ustad's advanced age. Almost tauntingly, he yells back, like a man possessed, '*Tora, tarana*!'

The Ustad has no choice but to return to his *tarana*. The *tabalachi* begins his rapid *upaja* again. This time it is the Ustad who is in danger of losing the *sam*.

He looks pleadingly at Guruji. Before Guruji can join in and give the Ustad a temporary respite, like a thunderclap ricocheting off the walls, Prasanna Sinha exclaims, 'Why're you trying to sing with your *shagird*? If you want to join battle with me, do it alone.'

Sureshwari Devi now rushes to the stage. '*Tumse hua kya beta?*' What's come over you, son?' she asks the *tabalchi*. '*Yeh danda-baazi ka akhara nahi hai.* This isn't some arena for stick-fighting.'

The *tabalchi* is still lost in his reverie. He shakes his head and then feebly says, '*Abhi mom-batti jalna bahut baki hai.*' There's still lots of tallow on the candle.

'Are you trying to kill Ustadji?' Sureshwari says curtly. The *tabalchi*'s face grows sheepish and he drops his head. She continues, 'Do you know that a *tabalchi* died during a duel like this with Ustad Hafiz Khan? *Agar aisa chale to tumhara bhi kayamat aa sakta hai*! Even your death may be at hand if you continue like this! Now, quiet down and come back to your senses.'

'I'm sorry, *mujhe maaf kar dijiye*! Please forgive me. I don't know what happened to me,' the *tabalchi* says. Then, as we feel the tension that had been palpable throughout the hall begin to ease, he advances towards the Ustad and falls at his feet.

'*Koi baat nahi, beta.* No matter, son,' the Ustad replies, clasping the younger man to his breast. '*Aisa kabhi kabhi achanak ho jata hai.* Such things sometimes happen suddenly. *Yeh mere liye pahli baari nahi.* This isn't my first time, you know.'

The hall explodes into thunderous applause.

1.10

Ever since I have known him, travel has brought forth even more poetic raptures from Nazrul than music. I have seen this in myriad settings, on our boyhood trips with *Dadu* to the surreal beauty of Kanyakumari and the Rann of Kutch, and amidst the opulent palaces and forts and the magnificent *haveli*s rising from the desolate sandy plains of Jodhpur and Jaisalmer.

Perhaps Nazrul has always known how to free his soul, so to speak. To really give voice to the wanderlust typical of the Bengali heart, symptomatic of its craving for romance and chivalry and adventure, and its attempt to touch the glories of nature's marvels and man's creations.

Since our train has arrived on the proverbial *lalmati* or 'red soil' of Birbhum district on our way to the *Poush Mela* this morning, much to Prem Kishan's bemusement and mirth, Nazrul has been spouting bursts of poetry and song.

We have already visited the spectacular murals and frescoes of Binod Bihari Mukherejee, many several stories high and mostly done after he went blind. We have also marvelled at the iconic sculptures of Ramkinkar Baij and Somnath Hore which seem to arise straight from the red, rocky soil and fill the environs of the famous Kala Bhavan with an elemental power beyond the realm of words. And basked at the *'chatim-tala'* under the massive banyan tree in Bhuvandanga made famous by Maharshi Debendranath Tagore.

Now the day is half done and Nazrul still seems in a state of near-reverie. We are close to the central fairgrounds where the roving *baul* singers are performing amidst the vendors and the bustling stalls which have been set up all around for the rush of thousands of visitors. Even though it is hard to hear the philosophical words from afar, their inimitable lyricism and the longing and pathos in their enunciation are inescapable. As the day progresses, the crowds thronging the huge leather and handicrafts stalls, and the stalls vending dozens of traditional Bengali sweets and food from all corners of the country, grow steadily larger.

After lunch, as we walk towards the central fairgrounds again, two young girls dressed as Ma Kali stretch out pewter plates in front of us for alms. Our eyes then land on a handsome *baul* ducking behind a stall. He has a tall, spare frame covered in saffron robes and long tresses peeping out beneath the silk scarf wrapped around his head. 'My *moner manush*, the man of my heart!' Nazrul exclaims. 'Remember what the face-reader said.'

As Prem Kishan and I look at him in astonishment, he takes after the man. We follow him. Prem Kishan says impatiently, 'Come on, Nazrul! What're you up to, man? We're leaving town chasing after some unknown *sadhu*!'

Nazrul doesn't reply. There is now a sparkle in his eyes overlaying the dreaminess. As we come up on the lush greenery lining the ravines of the '*khoyai*' with deer prancing along the edges, the *baul* halts.

He wheels around and yells out in Bengali, 'What do you want, Nazrul? Why're you following me?'

Prem Kishan and I too halt in our tracks, startled. How does he know Nazrul's name? But Nazrul runs to him and collapses in a heap near the *baul's* feet before bursting into tears.

The *baul* strokes Nazrul's hair for a few minutes, and then says again, this time more softly, 'What do you want? Do you want to sing for me?'

Deciding this is invitation enough, Nazrul begins singing. '*Hari ke bhed na payo Rama, kudrat tori rangi birangi,*' he sings. 'I find no difference between Hari and Rama, your manifestations are multihued,' echoes off the desolate slopes of the famed *khoyai* ravine. But Nazrul does not stop with one song. He launches into Kabir's *bhajan* in Raga *Jogiya, Is tan dhan ki kaun barayi, dekhat naina mitti milai.* 'What is this pride about this body and wealth? Don't you see how they crumble to dust?' his voice soars.

The sombre strains of *Jogiya* seem to acquire an otherworldly air, some kind of transcendent gravity, as Nazrul hurls them onto the crags and quarries all around us. He has reached that stage of complete communion with the *khoyai*. As for me, I feel suspended in some other ether, transfixed both by the sound, as well as the beatific smile and closed eyes of the *Baul*.

When the song ends, the *Baul* opens his eyes and says, 'How beautiful is the play of Allah, the *leela* of Krishna. They are in your every note. Tell me, *beta*. What do you want of me now?'

'I want your blessings, *baba*,' Nazrul whispers.

However, the *Baul* declares, 'I will come to you at an hour of great need. What do you need blessings from me now for? You have the blessings of the god of music. You'll hold the world in thrall with your singing. All of India will sway to your tunes. Go, go. That's all you need for now.'

Nazrul begins to ask, 'But what does that mean *baba*? The face-reader told me…'

'Yes, yes, I know,' the *Baul* interrupts. 'About your *moner manush*, the man of your heart. But this is enough for now. Everything will reveal itself in good time.' And then, raising his hand in greeting towards all of us in turn, he strides off.

Nazrul rises and attempts to brush the filth off his clothes, but there is not a speck of dust anywhere on them. As we stare at each other in astonishment, the *Baul* returns, 'I forgot to mention,' he says, 'we will meet here tonight for a traditional night of communal singing. I want you to come – especially you, Nazrul.' Then, without waiting for a reply, he strides off again.

****

Prem Kishan is showing us yet another side of his multifaceted personality. On a dare from Nazrul, he has taken up the challenge of passing off as one of the myriad *sadhus* thronging the fair. He appears to have neither the slightest fear nor any of the inhibitions that might grip any other sane person forced into such conning with high-stakes.

As we watch, he takes a seat on the mat which he has hurriedly purchased from a nearby stall together with the flowing saffron robes in which he is now dressed. He has chosen a location beside a large rock on one corner of the fairground. The rock is partly buried and he begins hacking away near the bottom with a shovel borrowed from a nearby stall.

By the time he has exposed the base, we realise his grasp of human psychology, or at least of the mindset of those who flock to the religious fairgrounds of India. A sizeable crowd gathers around, watching him.

He looks up from his digging, wipes the sweat on his brow with the palm of his hand and says, 'Does any of you want this stone? Or a piece of it?'

No one answers. Nor does anyone raise their hand or step forward.

Prem Kishan returns to his shovelling. Moments pass. He rises again to speak. 'Do you understand now why I was digging up this stone?' His tone has assumed a measure of gravity and authority.

A voice from the crowd cries out, 'Because you were told to in a dream.'

Prem Kishan remains silent. He makes no response whatsoever.

Sometime later, perhaps fifteen minutes, someone drags a hose over from the next row of stalls. 'Can I wash it, *guruji*?' he says. 'Maybe that'll bring me good fortune.'

Prem Kishan leans over and whispers something into the man's ears. Then, as the man scurries to pick up the hose, he casts a meaningful glance in our direction.

About half an hour later, a small group of people approach our friend, now apparently deep in meditation beside the rock. We see them circle him for some time. And then, as he opens his eyes, we hear them ask, '*Baba*, may we pray here?'

Prem Kishan nods gravely.

In the following minutes, the stone is smeared with a paste of oil and sandalwood and vermilion. Incantations resonate around us, mingling with the smoke from the incense sticks which the devotees have lit. Prem Kishan is immersed in meditation, motionless in the lotus pose with a face straighter than an arrow.

Gradually, the 'devotees' begin disappearing. After they leave, Prem Kishan rises and comes towards us. A broad smile wreathes his lips. Then, as he reaches us, he gives us long, mischievous wink. '*Kya bhai?*' he tells Nazrul. 'What did I tell you?'

'*Maan gaye, bhai,*' Nazrul replies, gesturing to him as though taking off an imaginary hat from his head and bowing low in obeisance. 'I accept, brother. *Tu such-much bare kamala ki cheez hai.*' You're truly an amazing specimen.

Prem Kishan pats him on the back, '*Maan gaye na, sale!* You admit it then!'

****

On Christmas Day today, we attend the traditional evening service held in Tagore's beautiful Prayer Hall within the Shantiniketan University campus. We follow the winding queue into the candle-lit central area, with its stained glass and wrought iron prayer hall. The carols and hymns played by the staff and students and the readings from many religious traditions move several people in the congregation to tears.

****

Later, it is time for a traditional *Baul* community singing ritual, a platform for a musical debate and discussion on *Baul* philosophy. The *Bauls* have split into rival groups, one assuming the role of the disciple and the other the guru.

Before the singing commences there is an exhibition of *dhol*-dancing. I have of course seen *dhak* and *dhol* drummers at the neighbourhood *puja pandals* in Calcutta during Durga and Saraswati Puja. But this dance is something else altogether, hypnotic in its intensity, with the colourful costumes and masks accentuating the breath-taking choreographed leaps. The tones of the drums of different sizes resonate in our bodies, from the bass that shakes us to our core, to treble tones that speak an elemental language of their own. The fusion of the percussion and movement are an immediately intoxicating, never-to-be-forgotten jolt, an instant high.

Then, lamps are lit and the *Bauls* sit in a large circle, smoking *ganja* and tuning their instruments. Invocatory songs begin, growing into an impassioned wailing of the names of Radha and Krishna.

A debate begins with a *Baul* from one group rising to taunt the other group who are still smoking their *chillums*.

'Know also that thousands of "mad ones"
Smoking *ganja* endlessly
Do not get anywhere!'

An intoxicated member of the other group rises and, drawing on his chillum, responds,

'Come, come, O brothers!
All who want to smoke the *ganja* of love!
Can one who smokes the *ganja* of love
Really get high on anything else?'

Nazrul's *moner manush*, who has been sitting in the middle of the circle, rises and advances in our direction. He puts his arms around Nazrul. Pointing to the young *Baul* who is now standing, he says, 'This is the second *pravarta*, stage, following initiation. Listen to what he says.'

The *Baul* sings,
'O mind, be like a woman!
Assuming the nature of woman,
Practice your *sadhana*.
The body's passion will rise.'

As the singing continues in this manner of taunt and retort, Prem Kishan whispers, 'How much longer do we want to watch?'

'I want to stay till the end,' Nazrul replies. 'Why don't you return? I'll come later.'

Prem Kishan and I return to our guesthouse. When I awake the next morning, there is already a warm glow in the eastern sky, and I hear Nazrul coming up the steps to the room. He is singing under his breath,

Sudipto Roy Choudhury

'There is no use hiding my madness anymore;
I have lost all sense of time and place.
In bliss my mind dances;
Its bells ring day and night.

'Mad, mad…everyone is mad.
Why then rebuke the mad?
With an open mind, look within.
See if anyone is free of madness.

Some are mad for riches,
Some about themselves,
Some because they haven't enough,
Some for the taste,
Some for the form;
Some are mad in love.
Some just cry and laugh.
Madness has many forms.

Everyone says, "Mad, mad."
Is it the fruit of a tree?

1.11

Two days later, we are standing outside the main festival marquee in the school compound. Nazrul has been missing since this morning. And just minutes ago, Sureshwari Devi has triumphantly informed us that he has eloped with Rita Mahalanobis. Perhaps this is why he was singing of 'his mind dancing in bliss.'

This is just what Sureshwari Devi has been angling for all along, almost goading the couple into something of this sort on every possible occasion over these past months. But I still cannot believe that Nazrul has actually gone ahead and done it. Then there is, of course, the issue of the Mahalanobis family's reaction.

Expectedly, Mr. Madan has rushed off to pacify them, to douse the flames before they leap sky-high. They are an influential family and their anger could easily set the school ablaze. Lopa has joined us a short while ago. I glance quickly at her face, attempting to gauge her reaction. But it is quite impassive. Idanbai's lips are squeezed into a thin, red line with not even a hint of her usual smile. She is not chewing her usual *paan* either.

'Let's go inside,' Guruji says after some time. 'We need to come up with a course of action. Of course everything depends on how the Mahalanobises take the whole affair.'

As we make for the door of the school, Mr. Madan enters the gate and comes rushing back in our direction. 'Let's wait for him, see how the Mahalanobises reacted,' says Guruji. Idanbai now reaches for the *paan-daan*, just as Mr. Madan comes up to us. His face is drawn. Idanbai squints and then puts a toothpick in her mouth.

'They're certainly not taking it too well,' Mr. Madan tells us slightly breathlessly. 'But they're quite calm. I managed to dissuade them from calling the police.'

'But why the police?' Sureshwari Devi asks, showing her first sign of unease. 'After all, they're two adults. And no crime has been committed. They should know that such things have always happened in the music world.'

We all walk into the main performance hall and settle down on the *dhurree*-lined floor. Even after the tea and samosas are brought in, the uneasy silence lingers. Everyone is pensive. Sureshwari Devi is staring down at her nails. In the corner, Mr. Madan and Guruji are confabulating in whispers. And Lopa and Idanbai are sitting quietly some distance away.

Finally Mr. Madan rises, saying, 'I'll see whether there's any more news. And what the Mahalanobises are planning.'

After he leaves, Guruji points to his trusty gramophone with its dented horn and the old-fashioned needles and records which he steadfastly refuses to give up, and asks, 'Music anyone? Or have we already had too much for the day?'

When no reply comes, he moves Nazrul's *swar-mandal*, leaning on the wall next to the gramophone to the corner. As his fingers brush the strings, ravishing tones softly blanket the room as though Nazrul is here with us in person. A few minutes later, the strains of '*Jamuna ke teer*' on the gramophone take their place.

'Abdul Karim Khan,' says Sureshwari Devi. 'He eloped with a relative of his patron, Maharaja Sayajirao of Gaekwad, didn't he?'

'Yes, and the writ of British law didn't run in the princely states then. So the Maharaja could even have had him shot, had he been caught,' Guruji says, nodding.

There is a sudden snapping sound. Idanbai stands. She goes over to the corner, spits out the broken toothpick and walks out of the room. She is quite dignified, but there is no mistaking her manner. This last bit of conversation has taken things beyond her tolerance.

Sureshwari Davi stands up as well. 'I have to prepare for this evening's performance,' she says. Idanbai's stalking out of the room appears to have restored her earlier equanimity.

1.12

On the final evening of the festival, the atmosphere is once again electric, following a spirited instrumental *jugalbandhi* ending the afternoon session. And expectations are running sky-high.

Sureshwari Devi is to begin the evening's proceedings. She is again wrapped in trademark white silk, with diamonds flashing in her ears and nose. I marvel at her composure. There is no hint of the turbulence surrounding Nazrul's elopement from earlier in the day. 'I suppose it comes from generations of performing,' I think to myself.

She has chosen a *sarangi* alongside the *tanpura* for accompaniment. As she begins by matching her voice to the *tanpura* in the time-honoured way of using the pure *aah* or *shuddh aa-kaar*, the whole hall seems to come to throbbing life. What resonance and what purity of *swara*! As I exclaim softly, Prem Kishan says, 'She'll certainly be hard for me to follow. There's years of *riyaz* behind this.'

'Generations actually,' I say.

As she proceeds, as always, I marvel at the perfection, the detail and flawless execution of each phrase, every part of the *bahalwa*, and the subtle interplay between the two *madhyams* or fa-notes that immediately set up the character of the *raga*, almost like a tangible presence.

As usual for the Jaipur school, the *raag vistaar* is relatively limited. But then she begins to weave the magic carpet of *taans* for which her *gharana* is famed. What variety and spectacular colours they come in! And what breath control!

The *tabalchi* is playing a very slow or *ati vilambit tin-taal*, and the *taans* take flight from various intermediate points. The patterns are so finely woven that each *taan* is followed by a *mukhda* lasting only one full beat or so. Their *chalan* or progression grows increasingly intricate, and yet the notes remain bell-like in clarity and execution. Each progression spins like a child's rotating fireworks, sometimes touching a note for an instant a shade more stridently, before making a new convoluted *phirat* every time and returning to the *mukhda*.

This is the handiwork of some magician composer, two-dimensional both in intent and execution, like the perfect fusion of gems into metal in the most intricate *jadwa* or *mina* jewellery.

As she finishes, Sureshwari Devi rises to her feet, barely lifting her head and smiling, and then nodding slightly to acknowledge the standing ovation that continues for a full five minutes.

Then, as soon as the applause fades, she launches into the famous *thumri* of the Banaras school, *Sajna ghar mere ji na lage bin tere*. Such is the power of the rendition, the variation of phrasing and tone and emphasis, that, after a few minutes, each time she returns to utter *Ji na lage* with a caressed, differently inflected, improvisation ranging between a sigh and a wail, many of the spectators in front of us, most of them men, wipe their eyes with their handkerchiefs.

"Too much more of this and I'll be knocked out even before entering the ring tonight.' Prem Kishan whispers. 'Closing out a festival like this can be injurious to one's reputation, I see.'

'Wait till you hear her *ghazals* and *kajris* and *chaitis*. If she really warms to it, she can put anyone out of business for the evening. She's not the reigning *ghazal* queen, perhaps even the best in recent times, for no reason,' I say to a visibly nervous Prem Kishan.

1.13

On the evening of the following day, the festival is finally over and most of the out-of-town musicians have departed. What with the month-long preparations for the festival, the continuous buzz of activity and the musical highs while it lasted, and the drama surrounding Nazrul and Rita on the last day, I feel that a tidal wave has passed over us.

In the lawn, the decorator's crew are folding the marquee cloth into large rolls and stacking them atop the piles of bamboo stakes which have been dug out of the ground. I step inside through the main door only to collide painfully with a metallic object. Guruji rushes towards me, 'It's Babuji, Aniket. He's been so cooped up this past week. I didn't have time to care for him. So I put him out to sun. I hope the cage didn't cut your head or face.'

'It's all right, Guruji,' I say, sizing up his pet parrot still rocking from side to side in its suspended enclosure.

Tea is brought in, accompanied by delicious rose-water flavoured *rajbhogs*, *chandrapulis* emitting the aroma of molasses and sultana-flavoured coconut, and the cauliflower *samosas* and savoury *hing* or asafoetida-spiced *kachoris* that appear in the city's sweetshops every winter. But there are also European pastries. 'These're from the new Kathleen's outlet outside Gariahat Market,' Guruji tells me. 'Now we have really good pastries in south Calcutta, not just these local imitations. No need to go to central Calcutta anymore.'

But my mind is not really on the food. In fact, the surfeit of snacks only reminds me of the reason I am here. Idanbai has asked to see me with no delay. And she has expressly requested that Guruji be present.

We switch on the TV. Calcutta Doordarshan is screening the film *Chowringhee* based on Mani Shankar Mukherjee, or Shankar's classic novel of the same name. At precisely the heart-stopping instant when Gomez, the leader of the hotel band, breaks into *Que Sera Sera, Whatever will be, will be*, my heart actually skips a beat. It is the doorbell. 'I bet it's an omen, Guruji,' I say. He smiles reassuringly at me and rises to open the door.

Fifteen minutes later, we are seated around the centre table. We have sipped our tea and munched on the snacks in near-silence. Except for her usual courteous initial greeting, Idanbai has been silent the entire time.

Even so, I have been unable to keep my gaze off Lopa. Her eyes are downcast and she looks listless and dejected. But she has worn the beautiful terracotta costume jewellery set I have brought back for her from the *Poush Mela* – with various poses of a dancer engraved in black on a turquoise background on all the panels of the necklace and earrings. Does that mean that she has decided to stand up to her mother?

Now Idanbai clears her throat and looks up at Guruji.

'Vishnu, you know why I asked you to arrange this meeting,' she says.

'Yes Idan,' Guruji says softly. 'But are you sure that what you want is the right thing? For them?'

'I only know the ways of the music world, Vishnu. You know how Gauharjaan, the light of Calcutta's music world, was reduced to selling *bandishes* for a rupee per head after falling for an Afghan wanderer. Or how Siddheshwari Devi never outlived the stigma of having eloped with a local prince in her teens.'

'But those days are long gone, Idan. Things are changing now. You see how everything all around us is evolving. You know this. We talk about it all the time.'

'I only know what I went through because of –,' Idanbai stops herself. 'You know, Vishnu. The codes of the music world have always been harsh and unforgiving.'

'But auntie,' I interject, 'I don't care for those codes. And things can't be that rigid. Codes evolve and change. Even in the music world. And we're part of the world at large too, aren't we?'

'Auntie, auntie,' Babuji the parrot interrupts, repeating a familiar word.

Idanbai raises her hand, but does not even look at me. 'Aniket *beta*, I beg you. For both of your sakes, for my sake, please let us be.' Her voice has dropped to a hoarse whisper. There is no anger in her tone. Just entreaty and a hint of a sob. And fear. This is no make-believe. I sense apprehension behind her words.

I look at Lopa and then at Guruji. Both are sitting silently, eyes downcast.

And then I feel anger. A terrible burning coursing through me like a flame. 'Come on, Lopa,' I say. 'Say something for God's sake! For your sake, for our sakes.' I am almost shouting now and I register the shock on everyone's faces. This screaming is not like me.

'*Beti*, do you want to say anything?' Guruji asks Lopa gently.

Lopa's face is ashen and tears are glistening on her eyelashes. But she doesn't say anything. Not a single word.

We sit in silence. And then Idanbai rises to her feet. Guruji walks over to Lopa and folds her in his arms. He nods towards Idanbai.

Then he turns towards me and says, '*Beta*, you're dearer to me than any son. Your *dadu* was the truest soulmate of my life. And I've seen Lopa grow up from the time she was a tiny thing. I know that this is not right for the two of you.'

Idanbai says, and there is now a hint of irritation or perhaps aggression stemming from insecurity in her voice, 'Vishnu, you are our dear friend and protector. But this has to be our decision – Lopa's and mine alone. After what happened yesterday with Nazrul and Rita, I... we have no other choice. No choice whatsoever.'

'This will always be your decision. Yours and Lopa's,' Guruji says quietly. Does he mean me and Lopa, or Idanbai and Lopa? Perhaps he has intentionally phrased it ambiguously to disguise his intent. Then he shakes Lopa gently by the shoulders and adds, 'But never forget, Lopa, never forget the legends of Ghosha and Lopa that I told you. And the story of the whispered *raga*, Aniket.'

Tears stream down Lopa's face profusely. But she still doesn't say anything.

After an interminable silence, Idanbai says, 'Come *beti*,' drawing Lopa towards her. '*Chal, ab jana chahiye.*' Come, we should go now.

As Guruji waves them goodbye, I surprise myself by saying, 'Goodbye auntie.' My voice feels disembodied. It takes all of my strength to keep it from trembling and to keep my tone neutral.

'Goodbye auntie,' echoes Babuji, rocking his cage animatedly from side to side as the door closes after them.

1.14

Five months later, Nazrul and Rita return and things begin settling back to normal after their marriage. But Idanbai shows no change of heart. In all this while, I have only managed to talk to Lopa a couple of times. As I enter the school courtyard, I see Guruji on the ground floor verandah. I have just returned from the American Consulate on Harrington Street, recently re-christened to Ho Chi Minh Sarani after the Vietnam War.

'So how did the interview go? Did you get the visa?' Guruji asks rising from his chair and rushing anxiously towards me. He is getting on, but long years of discipline, including rigorous routines of both yoga and *pranayama* have kept him lithe and fit.

'Yes, yes, Guruji. It was very smooth. The visa officer didn't ask me almost any questions,' I say.

'What did he say? Tell me. Tell me the exact words.'

'He just asked me my rank in the electronics engineering batch, and when I said third, he said, "Come back at 3.30 in the afternoon."'

'As simple as that,' Guruji says with a smile and tears in his eyes. 'I guess they know what they're getting.' He emits a long sigh and says, 'So this is it. This is how it is to be, *beta*!'

I know the unspoken anguish behind his words for where things are leading and for what might have been. And the worry.

But I have no answer. Maybe there are no answers in such situations in life.

I try to joke, to feign an enthusiasm that I do not feel. 'Yes Guruji. I'm really looking forward to it. They said that there'd be an orientation session for all students at the consulate next month.'

Guruji merely says, 'Go then, *beta*. Maybe you will see things better from afar. Sometimes it is the only way. Even if it's only to come back home later.'

I attempt to respond to him but my tears choke my words.

'Life can be so hard, *beta*. Maybe even more in this poor land of ours – so low have we fallen. I had such hopes for you.' He embraces me, openly weeping now.

As we stand embracing each other, I say, 'Don't worry, Guruji. Everything will be all right. I still have you. And Nazrul. How many people are so blessed?'

'If only I could believe that, *beta*. If only I could tell you that this seems right to me.' He falls silent, his shoulders hunched in a gesture of worry.

After several minutes, he looks up. 'I expected so much of you, *beta*. We all did. I only pray that this is your true compass. Your Pole Star.'

MAJH (MIDDLE)

Ithaca, New York, 1995

Whom have you left behind, oh mind, oh my mind?

Life passes, but you have no peace, oh mind,
oh my mind.

You've now forgotten the path by which you left –

How will you return to her door, oh mind,
oh my mind?

— Rabindranath Tagore

2.1

'Do we have all the food? Your student went to Elmira and Syracuse for the cake and the Indian sweets. Is he back yet?' I ask Prem Kishan. 'We'll have to get going to the airport soon to pick everyone up, and there's still some setting up to do at the Cornell Music Department before the concert.'

'Relax, *yaar*' Prem replies in his usual drawl. He arrived this afternoon from New York City. True to his youthful ambitions, he immigrated in the late seventies, initially eking out a living by waiting on tables in Soho and Greenwich Village, before assuming the more lucrative *avatar* of Indian godman-cum-vocal performer. That has led to his current directorship of the largest school of Indian music in New York City.

There is a knock on the door. 'The *biryani*, *kababs* and the main dishes are all here from Kohinoor,' Prem yells out from the front door moments later.

'Good,' I say. 'I've put out the plates and silverware. And the nuts and *chikis*. We can re-heat the *samosas* with the *kababs* when we return after the performance and then put them out. How're you doing with the drinks?'

'I've put the vodka, ouzo and tequila out. And the red wine's chilling as well, *yaar*. I put out the wine glasses there on the kitchen table. Is that okay?'

'Yup, that's great. I think we just need some napkins and I'll fill the filter jug for the water. And leave a note to myself to not forget the ice. They'll ask for it anyway.'

'I didn't think you'd have an Indian restaurant in such a small place, *yaar*.'

'Oh, there're several. Ithaca has a yuppie population, so they're always willing to try new things. And Indian food's hardly a novelty in the US anymore. Not like the early seventies when Diwali dinners for the Indian Student Association meant gangs of students chopping mounds of cabbage and cauliflower, not to mention crying over heaps of diced onions and cursing as our hands burnt from slicing bags of green chilies.'

'Oh, I've done things like that too,' says Prem. 'Now what's all this about this new singer, Niloy or whatever his name is?'

'He's not that new at the school any more. But he's the director's blue-eyed boy. Looks well-set to topple Nazrul from his perch any day now. But he apparently has a thing with the bottle. A running love-affair. Except that he almost passes out when he overdoes it, and creates real scenes on stage.'

'So Guruji warned you to keep an eye on him?'

'Yes, but I'll be running around, so I want you to mark him closely. Or at least keep an eye on him at all times. If he so much as goes near a bottle before the concert, I want you to stick to him like a leech. Guruji said that a good trick is just to dilute his whiskey with lots of water. After a few, he doesn't even know the difference. And keep him talking and keep the munchies coming.'

'Consider it done,' Prem says. '*Yaar*, I'll *chipko* to him like his shadow.'

The Whispered Raga

'D'you want a drink now?' I ask.

'I noticed you've been drinking quite a bit,' Prem says, raising an eyebrow. 'I don't remember you this way before.'

'I'll tell you some other time,' I say, jumping to my feet and walking to the window. The piles of virgin snow, rimmed by the dirtier patches of salt and footprints, are reminders of the season's first big storm that hit the previous day. As is usually the case in Ithaca and the parts of northern New York state which lie in the snow belt, the sky is a dull, leaden grey. Mirrors my mood perfectly.

Turning away from the bleak exterior, I begin pacing up and down the room. It is some time before I became aware that Prem is watching me. 'You're very tense and restless, *yaar*,' he says. 'You sure everything's okay? This isn't the Aniket I knew back in India.'

'I'll tell you someday. Don't worry, I'll live.' But the outward flippancy only serves to highlight my inner sense of ennui, the continuous dull apathy which has become my daily companion.

'OK, *yaar*. Only don't be shy. I'll go and pick up the *samosas* then. Should be back within forty-five minutes from what you told me.'

'Thanks Prem. I'll wait for the call from the Music Department, and then we can hit the road for the airport as soon as you're back.'

After he leaves, I turn back to the window. From the left corner, behind the screen of snow-laden branches, the long curve of the shoreline of the Cayuga Lake is dimly visible even in this cloudy haze. Strings of coloured lights have been hung from the homes bordering the water. Far in the distance, across a long stretch of the lake, giant illuminated letters pierce the gloom, mockingly flashing the message 'Merry Christmas' in my direction.

This is my sixteenth winter in Ithaca. After graduate and post-doctoral work in Boston and Arizona, I had been more than fortunate to land a position in Cornell's applied mathematics programme. Many of my peers had fared far worse, especially in those early years of the Reagan administration, when government budgets for civilian science and humanities programmes had faced deep cuts to allow for massive rises in defence spending and huge tax cuts for the super-wealthy and corporations who were the real constituency for his government and party.

My wife of the time, through an arranged marriage, and I chose this house in Cayuga Heights, both for its beautiful location near the long, 'finger' lake which gave the area its name, as well as its proximity to both the University and good schools. And the greenery which still dots the area, though a far cry from the lush foliage and deep ravines and gorges criss-crossing the campus proper, are a soothing sight to the eyes during the all-too-short summer season.

When my marriage fell apart, through incompatibilities which had been long-evident but had been brought to a head by the pressure-cooker in which tenure- earning faculty in this prestigious institution inevitably found themselves, I stayed on.

Ithaca has gradually become my home away from home. The relentless pressure of the early years has gradually morphed into a more orderly, though hectic lifestyle. With tenure and experience, the research ideas flow more easily. There are more grants, and the ensuing stream of graduate students and post-docs pick up the slack created by my having slowed down from the earlier, frenetic pace.

Culturally and intellectually, Ithaca is one of the most stimulating small towns in the US. With faculty and students drawn from all over the world and a relentless whirl of lectures, concerts and art films, it rivals any place except perhaps the world's greatest cosmopolitan cities in the fare for the mind on offer.

And with the Finger Lakes, the Catskill Mountains, the forests and slopes of the Adirondacks, Niagara Falls, as well as New York, Toronto and even Montreal within easy driving distance, my holiday calendar is also always chock-a-block with trips and activities.

In the way typical of the US, a slew of various activities has gradually enlarged my circle of friends, almost swelling my telephone book to bursting with cards and post-its. Membership of the Cornell Folk Dancers, the hiking club, the India Association and sundry other campus activities pleasantly fill up the leisure hours. And the activities and friendships through the Film Club and History Association more than rival those I had known in the various film associations and cafes during both my IIT and graduate school years.

And yet, there has always been a gnawing sense of loss. Like all NRIs, indeed all immigrants, there is an emptiness. As though a large part of oneself had been excised. 'Surgery without anaesthesia' is the graphic description a fellow

NRI gave during one of the India Association's Hindi film screenings. It is the actual loss of India, of the parent culture in its totality, not just of family and friends and familiar surroundings, which underlies that aching void.

But the thing I miss most of all, the subject closest to my heart, the one which I so casually spurned so many years ago, is Indian classical music. There is some interest in the Music Department, but understandably enough, it doesn't run very deep.

By virtue of Cornell's exclusivity, Ithaca's NRI circle is a handpicked one, and thus naturally sheltered from some of the surreal episodes arising from cultural displacement which one sees in immigrant ghettos in the larger American cities. It has always offered me warm hospitality. Indeed, it is a haven, a veritable life-saver during the dull evenings of the longer Christmas and summer breaks, when, as we are often wont to joke, 'dogs and groups of Indian and Chinese students' are the only people one sees on the deserted streets. Predictably enough though, in this community primarily composed of scientists and engineers, Indian classical music is at best a serious hobby.

Even though I have many friends belonging to diverse circles, and even more acquaintances, there is no one I can open my heart to without restraint. No friend who is like my brother, as Nazrul had been. And no one like Lopa!

Occasionally there is a letter or a card from Nazrul. He has been a star, both in the school and nationally, for many years now. But there has been no diminution in either his effusiveness or his warmth towards me. For some years, I even copied articles featuring Nazrul from the Times of

India in the University's main Olin Library. That was in the old days (before the days of PCs and the widespread information diffusion on the Internet) when the paper would arrive a fortnight late, only to be immediately snapped up by a pair of Indian hands and then devoured by an even hungrier pair of eyes.

Lopa writes less and less frequently. She has sequestered herself in Lucknow at the Bhatkhande College, emerging only occasionally to perform. Certainly she has built a reputation, and is even occasionally invited to sing at the very best music conferences and festivals. However, she has not come close to fulfilling what many at the school had always considered her prodigious potential, greater perhaps than even Nazrul. She rarely writes anything about herself, except in passing. Her letters are usually a litany of daily activities. True to her innate reserve, things of a personal nature in her letters mainly concern her mother Idanbai who has been ailing in Calcutta.

During my early years in the US, including the first few years in Ithaca, the collapse of my marriage and the lack of really close friendships hadn't mattered so much. In a mobile society, it is easy enough to launch oneself like a perpetually spinning top into an endless whirl of activity, with work and fun, weekdays and weekends, merging into one continuous blur. Almost half of my life and most of my adult years have now been spent in this manner.

It is also not hard to rationalise away the missing things or the blue moods that increasingly seem to settle like a fog on my mind on Sunday afternoons. One needs to be an optimist, after all, to see the glass half full and not half empty. And don't really close friendships get harder to come by with the years? Everyone, of all nationalities and cultures, seems to be agreed on this. Not to mention the fact that we are blessed to be surrounded by youth, and to be in an atmosphere where one automatically makes friends from diverse backgrounds and age groups.

And there have been the affairs. The short ones, and the long-term one with the Puerto Rican faculty member from the Department of Education that had almost ended in marriage. But none has endured. Some have left a bitter after-taste. Perhaps, it is me. Maybe, I am a born misogynist, or perhaps just impossible to live with. And now the whole mating game has begun to pall. 'Been there, done that' is the cliché that increasingly comes to my mind when the familiar scenes of 'hitting on' or 'being hit upon' play themselves out at parties, or while dancing, or in bars.

There has also been the increasing sense of dissatisfaction with my work. Even though, paradoxically enough, the flow of ideas seems only to quicken, there is less and less challenge involved in the process of actual implementation. As I expertly play the academic system, farming out more and more details to others while keeping my productivity unimpaired, time has begun hanging heavy on my hands at the office. How does one pass one's time once the mandatory seven hours of teaching a week are done? I have only been at this publishing game for fifteen years. What does one do with the rest of one's professional life? One can only drink so much coffee. And haunting the hallways to chat up one's colleagues or visiting the campus store can hardly be expanded to a daily, full-time activity. Perhaps that's why aging academics increasingly sign up for committees and administrative work.

The Whispered Raga

But the first real sign of trouble, the feeling that all of the things that made up my adult life might no longer be enough, came one sleepless night in a hotel room in Florida. As the waves washed up on the sand in the brilliant moonlight, for the first time, the question 'Why am I here?' suddenly, elementally, flashed across my mind. 'Is this auto-suggestion?' I wondered, something triggered by the pop psychology stories which pepper the pages of American newspapers and magazines, especially on weekends. In fact, I remember, as a graduate student, laughing at a similar image in a story where I had first encountered the term mid-life crisis.

But it hasn't gone away. Auto-suggestion or not, this incident has been followed by increasingly frequent dreams. Initially they were benign. Perhaps an image of a pop psychiatrist spouting pleasant platitudes on weekend TV. Or a smiling image of Swami Muktananda, like the ones adorning the front windows of both the Cornell and Borealis Bookstores, reaching out to bless me from the pages of his book *Where Are You Going*.

I could have survived that. But even that hasn't lasted. The nightmares that followed have been increasingly disturbing. And frequent. In fact, they alternate with episodes of insomnia. I have become paranoid about sleeping, of the next horrific image that will spring out at me from some phantasmagorical dream world the moment I close my eyes.

I have become like a jumping jelly-bean. And I am getting worse. The insomnia has begun to lead to blinding migraines. So, beyond the pill-popping has come the drinking. A peg each evening at first. Only to increase in peg-sized increments. Whatever it takes to drown the emptiness, the sense of the future yawning before me like some horrible monster. If only it would just snap me up into its jaws in one merciful bite.

I realise suddenly that I am pacing furiously up and down the room. This is another recent development. Its frequency has increased since the death of my aunt – my mother's sister – six months ago in Lucknow. Sometimes I pace back and forth in my office or at home for hours on end. Only exercise or yoga seems to help at such times.

I walk over to the window again. Perhaps a walk might calm the restlessness before Prem Kishan returns. But there are flurries outside. It looks pretty nasty already and it will be snowing hard again soon.

'Sing,' Guruji had said on the phone. Maybe I should give that a try.

I go into the second bedroom and take out the large Kashmiri *dhuree* bought from Calcutta's Central Cottage Industries all those long years ago. Laying it out on the floor, I begin my usual pre-music warm-up routine. A hundred push-ups, followed by the *simhasana* or lion pose from yoga. As I begin the *pranayama* routine of the full yogic breath, followed by *Kapalbhati, Bhrastika* and the cleansing breath, I feel the restlessness begin to subside.

'Maybe it'll work today,' I think, while performing the sweet voice *pranayama,* and finishing up with the *uddiyana* and *jalandhar bandhas.* But as I lie in the *shavasana* or corpse pose, instead of calm, the nervous energy begins to return, almost like a physical presence.

The Whispered Raga

Ten more minutes and I have taken out my beautiful old *tanpura* with its mother-of-*pearl* inlay. The strings are rusty and out of tune from disuse. A dash of WD-40 lubricant and some careful tuning, and I am set to go. But as I sound the first note, a wave of nausea sweeps over me. I utter an involuntary cry and push – nay, almost throw – the *tanpura* aside. And then sink beside it on the *dhuree*.

I don't know how long I remain in that position. But when I come to my senses, it is pitch dark outside. It is five-thirty, time to pick up the visitors from the airport in the rented van. As I hurry out after drawing the blinds and grabbing my parka and gloves, a spasm of fear clutches at my heart.

How will it feel to see everyone from the school after all these years? It had seemed the most natural thing in the world to suggest that they visit Ithaca, to do all the necessary legwork and make all the phone calls. Even last week, I had a sense of expectation, of an almost delirious happiness.

But why this nervousness now? Why should seeing Nazrul or Mr. Madan feel unsafe? After all, I saw them at regular intervals during my visits to Calcutta. Or is it the prospect of seeing Lopa again after all these years? But that is long past, over and done with.

Or maybe it is the prospect of them seeing me in my lair. What will they make of this life I have so painstakingly built? Is that the reason for my unease? Modern American life is all about optimising, of triangulating to find the best path among an often bewildering array of choices. What will they make of mine?

'I guess it's only natural to feel this way. I do value their opinion,' I think. But almost of its own volition, this is followed by the thought, 'Will they even begin to guess what it's cost me? And where I am now?'

2.2

Sensitive as always to the moods and colours of nature, Nazrul has chosen *Raga Darbari* to mirror the sombreness of the Ithaca winter evening. 'Perhaps it's a portent,' I think but catch myself. 'Bunkum. Just my imagination.'

The musicians are onstage, tuning their instruments. A murmur of anticipation passes through the audience with the ravishing strains emerging in waves as Nazrul twists the keys of the *swar-mandal*, its strings and chrome frame gleaming in the stage lights. Then, as the tones begin to hush, he turns intently towards the window. He alternately closes and opens his eyes, pausing a few seconds in each position, in his familiar gesture of communing with nature before the start of a programme.

Mr. Madan suddenly rushes to the stage. He whispers into Nazrul's ears, and the latter's brows furrow, maybe in annoyance of having his concentration broken or maybe not. I know that there is little love lost between them. They exchange some words, then Madan steps offstage and the first notes begin to invade our senses.

As Nazrul completes the rousing finale an hour later, the audience rises as one man. He stands, gesturing to the *tabalchi* and harmonium player to rise as well. They join their palms across their chests, bowing repeatedly to acknowledge the applause.

The accompanists walk into the wings. The Director of Cornell Music School, Michael MacArthur, walks onto the stage. He motions to Nazrul, and, to renewed applause, they walk back to centre stage. The lights are still dimmed and the spotlight is firmly on Nazrul. I see him blink slightly in the glare and then, squinting to locate me, he waves in my direction.

I have been clapping all this while. As I open my mouth to add my cheers to the second round of cries of *'Kya baat, kya baat! Kamal kar diya!'* no words emerge from my mouth. Instead, I choke and gag.

I quickly squeeze out to the end of the row, waving to Nazrul. His eyes are following me and I can see surprise in them. I turn, run down the aisle, out into the lobby and then up the stairs all the way to the men's room. Sobs are racking my whole frame now.

I rush into a cubicle, tear strips of toilet paper to line the seat and squat. I want to scream. A primal cry of some long-suppressed agony seems to be pushing itself up my gullet. But I cannot let it out.

There are people coming into the men's room now, chattering and laughing. I brace myself with my hands on the cubicle walls, watching my knuckles turn into pale fists as my whole body shudders and I struggle to silence the sobs as tears roll like rivulets down both cheeks.

2.3

Backstage, Rita Mahalanobis is saying to Nazrul, 'They loved you tonight, Nazrul. You've raised the bar so high for me for tomorrow night.'

Nazrul smiles at her. To me, Rita says in her usual gushing manner, 'Oh Aniket, can I bring my *tanpura* over tonight to your place? Maybe, we can all sing a bit together.'

I am just about to quip about the quality of an inebriated musician's singing when Mr. Cyrus Madan, or 'the Director' as everyone at the school tells me he wishes to be addressed nowadays, comes rushing up from the wings. 'Oh, it's you, Aniket *babu*,' he says when he sees me. I nod a greeting and then step up to shake his outstretched hand. I haven't seen him during my last few trips to Calcutta and I notice how much the worse for wear he looks from our last meeting five years ago.

Out of the corner of my eye, I search for Lopa. As though we met just yesterday, Mr. Madan says, 'You're doing pretty well, I see, Aniket *babu*.'

'And so're you,' I say politely, even as I notice the bulging waistline peeping out from beneath his suit jacket.

'Oh, my job keeps me on my toes. And not just the school's business, but my corporate responsibilities as well. I hope the food will be light tonight.'

'Oh, medium probably. It's been catered by an Indian restaurant,' I say, looking down at the shining new *tanpuras*, as well as the *tablas* and Nazrul's *swar-mandal* lying to one side.

I am just reaching down to strum the shiny strings when I feel a hand on my shoulder. Nazrul pulls me up and clasps me to his breast. For some minutes, we just stand there laughing, murmuring 'Oh, it's great to see you. How is everything?' into each other's' ears.

And then, he pushes me back and asks, 'Why did you rush out like that after the performance, Aniket?' I remain silent, but he notices my puffed-up eyes. He takes me by the shoulders and shakes me. 'You've been crying. *Bhai*, what's up? Come on. Tell me. Tell your brother.'

'I'll tell you, Nazrul. While driving home tonight. It'll take some time,' I mumble.

Clasping me again by both shoulders, Nazrul says, 'Guruji told me to ask about you when we were leaving India. He said he was worried about you.'

'He said you weren't doing too well either, Nazrul. Has he heard you sing recently? You were absolutely divine, transcendentally beautiful. It's like you've flowered into everything that you once promised to be, or that we expected of you. I didn't know whether to laugh from the majesty of some parts, or weep at the pathos of others.'

'Thank you, Aniket,' Nazrul says. Then, after a short pause, he adds, 'I don't know whether Guruji's mentioned anything. Things aren't very good at the school. And everything's not well between me and Rita. You know about our difficulty in having children. But there have been other things recently. I'm not sure how much more of this I can take. Only Guruji knows about it. I haven't even told *Ammi.*'

I am about to say something when Mr. Madan materialises beside us with Rita and Prem Kishan in tow. Michael MacArthur and his Japanese wife Keiko Yajima, both faculty members at the Cornell Music School, stroll over to join us. 'I have a great idea for the school, Nazrul. You'll jump when you hear it,' Madan says breathlessly.

'Tell them later, Cyrus *yaar*. Let's discuss it at Aniket's,' Prem Kishan says. 'Where's Lopa, *yaar*?' he asks Nazrul. 'I haven't even said hi to her yet. And I'm starving.'

'She's probably rehearsing somewhere,' Rita says. 'Always acting the star.'

'She's there over behind those curtains, near the small stage,' Nazrul says quietly. 'Why don't you go fetch her, Aniket? You didn't have a chance to talk to her at the airport, and it's been ages since you met.' He pushes me gently, urging me on with his eyes.

The row of footlights near the front of the stage are still on. Lopa is standing next to them, singing a passage to a *sarangi* player who sits a short distance away. She is dressed in a mauve *salwar kameez* with a matching Kashmiri shawl. There are streaks of white in the hair now, but there is no mistaking her. Her striking resemblance to her mother has only grown more marked with the years.

As I watch, I wonder whether she has heard me approaching. The *sarangi* player motions in my direction and she looks around. A shy smile of welcome wreathes her lips as she advances towards me.

I take a few steps. And then stop a few feet from her. 'Hi Lopa, it's been so long. But you look well,' I say almost without thinking. Do I even know her any more, the person that she now is?

'Hi Aniket. Yes, it has been so long, hasn't it?' And then hurriedly she adds, 'This is Jahangir Khan, the school's new *sarangi* player.'

'They're waiting for us in the other corner,' I say. 'I think everyone's pretty hungry.'

As we approach the others, Nazrul hastens towards us and wraps us in a bear hug. 'It's been so long, Lopa and Aniket, since we were all together. Remember how we were the three musketeers.'

'It has, Nazrul. We used to be so young then. And so innocent,' Lopa says. Then, turning to me, she says, 'I wasn't sure you'd still be the same. The last time we met…' She trails off awkwardly.

'It was at the school. They were screening Shankar's *Chowringhee* on TV that night.'

'Yes, I remember.'

I stare outside, suddenly at a loss for words. The sheer sides of the cliffs lining the main gorge look ghostly in the fading wintry light streaming in from the picture windows. The hanging bridge – or suicide bridge, as it has been re-christened – sways violently in the gusts blowing in from the north. Suddenly, unaccountably, a scene from that fateful evening comes rushing back through the mists of time. Babuji exclaiming, 'Goodbye auntie,' and rocking his cage animatedly from side to side as the door closes after Lopa and Idanbai.

'I remember every single thing, Lopa, down to the tiniest detail. You were wearing a turquoise *salwar kameez* with Bengali *kantha* stitching, and terracotta ornaments I had brought back from the *Poush Mela*. With figurines of folk dancers and their instruments. I've thought about that day I don't know how many times. But I'm sure it's of no consequence to you.'

Noticing Lopa's silence, Nazrul quietly says, 'We have so much to talk about. But I think everyone's hungry. I just want to gather up my things before we leave.'

'Yes,' I say. We walk over to the others. To Prem Kishan and Michael Macarthur I say, 'Why don't you go ahead with Mr. Madan and Rita and Lopa? Nazrul and I will follow. You have the spare key, right Prem?'

2.4

The snow has turned to freezing rain outside. As Nazrul and I start putting the covers on the instruments, I say, 'It'll be really nasty out there.' Pointing to a solitary figure gingerly slithering across the accumulated sleet on the Hanging Bridge over one of Cornell's larger gorges on Beebe Lake, I add, 'At least we'll be driving, Nazrul. Imagine if we had to be out there on foot, slipping and sliding in this muck.'

'I sensed it even before the concert. The gathering gloom, the sombre seriousness. That's why I chose *Darbari* for the second piece in the concert, although it was still a bit early in the evening. It seemed more appropriate to the mood and surroundings,' Nazrul says.

'It certainly fits the season. And my mood. But you must tell me all about everything. What you said about the situation at the school. And between you and Rita.'

Nazrul looks up from his *swar mandal* that he has been putting away in his box. 'I will,' he says. 'Let's find a quiet time tonight. We really do need to have a heart-to-heart talk.'

'I thought I was the one with problems,' I say. 'You're the star, the national treasure. You never said anything before.'

'God knows I've tried everything,' Nazrul says. 'You know in India they treat us musicians sometimes like demi-gods. Not as much as film stars perhaps. But we're not supposed to have human failings, to have personalities, or lives, or problems.'

'Neither am I. I'm the good son who played the middle-class game. Played the system to the hilt – went to IIT and then Harvard. I'm not supposed to have feelings. Or a life. When I go back, I'm the successful role model that our aspiring classes look up to.'

'How about here? How's life here at Cornell? The audience today seemed fantastic.'

'It's a mixed bag as with anything. I have lots of friends. But no one to really share music with deeply. It's strange in a way. The mobility and achievement-orientation of the culture is so high that everyone's always busy or on the move, so it's very easy to find any number of activities and acquaintances. But harder to make real friends.'

'How about the NRIs, the Indians?'

'A mixed bag again. But they're not independent of the background. And some are pretty maladjusted, comfortable only in their Indian ghetto. It's hard to generalise and I try not to judge. We all live as we can and we all have our problems and blind spots. But I've found that it can be even harder to discuss either music or films in a serious way with NRIs.'

'Why's that, though? They should know more, at least about Indian music.'

'Yes and no. I think it's the work pressure partly, the struggle to make it. And a certain materialism. The house, the two cars, the talk about stocks and bone china. I'm sure you see it more and more in India too.'

'Oh yes. Yes of course. And even more so after liberalisation. The middle class is really on the make now.

Students lack the previous dedication. Everyone wants quick success on radio or TV or by recording something.'

'How's the school doing?'

'Not so hot. You know that the Bani Tirtha music school folded up. They're pulling down the cinema hall next to it too to build a shopping centre-cum-multiplex. Madan's always after us with some money-making scheme or the other. That's actually part of my problem too. I haven't adjusted as willingly to him as my great friend Niloy. Actually, I sang a bit more freely tonight because Niloy eventually decided to stay on in New York and give Ithaca the go by.'

He utters the name with slight emphasis. 'Coming from you, Nazrul, that sounds pretty damning to Madan and this Niloy. Things certainly don't seem well in the state of Denmark. But we really should go now,' I say. 'The others will be waiting.'

As we step out into the snow, there is a shrill screeching overhead. Looking up, we see a flock of Canadian cranes headed southwards towards warmer climes. It seems strange that they are migrating so late in the season. Framed in the light of the moon, they seem painted on the backdrop of the sleet-streaked sky.

Nazrul catches his breath and whispers, 'What an ethereal, majestic sight. A perfect compliment to *Darbari*. Maybe things'll begin looking up again after all.'

2.5

By the time we arrive, everyone is already digging into the food and drinks. Prem Kishan has made himself comfortable on the floor. As I propose turning up the heating, there is a chorus of protests, 'No, no, it's fine.' 'It's warm with so many of us here.' 'You'll see after you warm up a bit.' And so on.

I give everyone a tour of the house. When we return to the living room, in his usual expansive fashion, Prem has poured out stiff shots of whiskey and vodka big enough to knock out the unwary. Rita sidles up to him and begins making small talk.

'I feel over-dressed,' says Nazrul. 'This *achkan* and the heavy shawl are too much with the heating.'

'I do too,' says Lopa, removing her shawl.

'What're you looking at?' I say, as Lopa and Nazrul walk over to a picture hanging on the wall.

'That's a terrible, faded black and white picture of all you as teenagers. You all look like plucked chickens,' Rita says, sidling up, blissfully unaware of what resonances the picture might hold for us. 'Why not replace it by a swanking new one, in bright new colours?'

Prem Kishan comes over from the kitchen and takes a seat next to Michael and Keiko. Rita comes back from her inspection of the picture and sits down beside him.

'How come you never married, Prem?' she asks with her usual bluntness. Prem shrugs. No doubt the news of Prem Kishan's innumerable romantic dalliances hasn't made its way across the seven seas.

'It was a fantastic concert,' Keiko says, turning towards Nazrul. 'I'm so looking forward to tomorrow evening.'

'How about making it a yearly affair?' says Prem. 'That's how I gradually built up my popularity and base of students when I came to New York. And then one thing led to another. And, in a decade's time, there was sufficient demand to start a school.'

'And you became a guru as well. Of everything from meditation to raga rock to healing ailments with raga music,' I quip.

As Prem nods good-humouredly, Nazrul chimes in, 'Tell us all the details, Aniket. The lowdown on the great guru of raga music in New York City.'

'But what about my idea of an annual concert series or Indian music festival here in Ithaca?' Prem asks.

'That might be reasonable and doable,' says Michael thoughtfully. 'But don't expect everything and everyone to catch fire like they did in New York. Ithaca's just a small town after all, although a pretty special one.'

'That does sound like a good idea!' Mr Madan interjects. 'And Prem has the experience to make it happen. But let me suggest something else. India's changing, you know. Raga rock and all kinds of fusion music are becoming the rage all over the country.'

'Yes,' Prem says. 'So what? It's really long overdue.'

'You'd be just the right person to lead the school in that direction. You have experience with that sort of music and business savvy and experience in marketing as well.'

'What're you suggesting?' Prem says with suspicion.

'I'm proposing that you come over and spend half the year as co-director of the school,' Mr. Madan says.

'Oh, that does sound like a perfect move in today's market,' Rita bursts out in the fawning manner she usually adopts towards Cyrus Madan. I had forgotten how annoying that was, and I see that it still as grating now. 'Will you consider it, Prem? You really must. And it comes right from the top, the Director of the school himself,' she adds, touching Prem's forearm lightly.

Nazrul's face hardens slightly and he disappears into the kitchen. Lopa watches him impassively.

As the others burst into an excited discussion, I walk over to Nazrul. I can feel Lopa's eyes following me too. Nazrul shrugs his shoulders and grimaces slightly. I put my fingers to my lips and hiss 'Shh.'

He grins. 'Let's go out onto the verandah.'

'They call it a patio here,' I say as we head out into the chilly but secluded area.

'Such a load of bull,' says Nazrul. 'But so typically Madan.'

'Yes. But let's talk about more pleasant things.'

'I know Lopa wants to say something to you. But you guys have left it so very late.'

I open my mouth, only to shut it as I see Cyrus Madan emerge on the patio. 'Thought I'd catch a smoke. Lord knows I need a fag, my little white stick of life,' he says.

We take seats on the chairs but jump back up with a yelp. 'It's bitterly cold, isn't it?' says Cyrus Madan.

'Yes,' I say. 'You probably should choose a different time of the year, maybe the fall or spring, if the Ithaca concerts really become annual affairs.'

We stand in silence for a few minutes, staring out into the gloomy chill as Mr. Madan lights his cigarette. 'How would you like to join us for tomorrow morning's rehearsal, Aniket?' Nazrul breaks in. 'Would that be all right, Cyrus?'

Mr. Madan grunts amiably. 'He's part of the family right, Aniket *babu*? What d'you think of my proposal to Prem Kishan?' he adds. Seeing my hesitation, he continues, 'It is a different world, Aniket *babu*. The purists of your youth will frown, no doubt. Anyway, no one ever understands anything I do. If I'd known myself what I was letting myself in for and how problematic the financial end might be, given the changing tastes of the public, I'm not sure I'd ever have taken up the school.'

'I'm sure you don't regret it,' I say.

'No, not really. At least not most of the time. All I'd thought was that we needed to preserve this A-grade school. And we've always had an association with the music world.'

'But surely the future isn't raga rock, or East-meets-West, or blends of modern Indian with classical music!' Nazrul cries.

'But that's exactly what most people want, Nazrul,' Mr. Madan says jovially. 'And we must evolve or die.'

'Oh, I do see the writing on the wall,' Nazrul says, his voice straining with anger. 'Only it can't be right to convert a leading school in India to be a clone of one in New York. After all, there will always be purists, really knowledgeable listeners and critics in India.'

'We'll only go part of the way,' Mr. Madan says between puffs of smoke.

'I suppose you mean a mix of the new and the old pure styles. And both will survive, but they'll need to co-exist,' I say.

'Yes, exactly!' says Mr. Madan. 'But how about introducing me to some really rich Americans with a soft spot for India, Aniket *babu*? Or some NRI doctors with moolah to burn.' He winks conspiratorially at me.

'Prem Kishan's your man for that,' I say. 'And New York's the place.'

'Yes, exactly. That's why our school needs him. I know how to handle these rich donors. Massage their egos a bit and make them the feel like VIPs in the school. And they open their purses.'

'Oh, the NRI doctors and engineers would love that,' I break in hurriedly as I hear Nazrul hiss, 'Bloody philistine' under his breath. 'But let's go back in, shall we?'

****

Half an hour an hour later, Prem Kishan rises to his feet. 'I shall take my leave friends. It's been a wonderful evening with old friends, very nostalgic.' His words are beginning to slur. 'I suppose drink makes you more sentimental. Meeting you guys makes me want to go back to India and never come back again. But I've burnt my bridges, I suppose.'

'No, no, my friend,' says Mr. Madan, sensing a heaven-sent opportunity to press home his earlier proposal and turn on the full force of his directorial charm.

'That'll have to wait for now. I never rush into such things,' says Prem Kishan. 'And I've had a long day starting with the drive down from New York this morning. I need to sleep on it.'

'Not to mention all the whiskey you poured down your gullet,' I say with a chuckle.

'Yes, yes. Sleep on it. Think it over. It'll be mutually beneficial to both you and us. A true symbiosis,' Mr. Madan beams.

'I can see why you're the Director,' says Prem Kishan with a smile. 'Never miss an opportunity, do you?'

'I'll make you co-Director, just you see. Your name will become a byword in north Indian classical music circles. Just like I did for Rita here and our star male singer Niloy.' Madan is positively preening by now. And surely that last statement was meant as a snub to Nazrul, although he seems not to notice.

Michael and Keiko have also risen to their feet. Sensing that the party is winding down, Mr. Madan also rises. 'You will give me a ride, won't you, Michael?' he asks.

2.6

There is a long silence after they leave. Now two middle-aged men and two middle-aged women sit in the companionable glow cast by the flickering tongues of flame arising from the wood in the fireplace at the edge of the living room. As though signalling that everything is not as it appears, the silence is periodically punctuated by the howling gusts from the snowstorm gathering strength outside.

After some time, Lopa rises. 'I think I'll just go and stretch out on the *divan* in the small room in the corner,' she says. 'What do they call it here?'

'A den or family room, as opposed to the larger living room,' I reply.

'I think I'll join you,' Rita says. 'I thought we might sing a little. But it's late and everyone's pretty tired already.'

'Remember old times,' says Nazrul, casting off his slippers and reclining on the sofa as we watch them leave. 'We had so many hopes and dreams. My voice would hit the ultra-high register with no effort at all. And so would yours.'

'Not anymore,' I say. 'I can barely bring myself to sing.'

'We all need a second wind in life, don't we? The first gust weakens and begins to peter out. Maybe I should try and compose. Or try some of this East-meets-West stuff, or these new-fangled combinations of classical with Tagore and the like.'

'God knows I feel that way too. Just quitting or trying something completely new. But I'm like the proverbial *dhobi ka kutta, na ghar ka na ghat ka.*' I have just compared myself to the washerman's dog, no longer comfortable either at home or the *ghat*. 'Like all immigrants. What else could I do anyway? But you, you can do anything you choose to, Nazrul. You're a superstar.'

'I wish it was that easy, *bhai*. The public expects newer and newer wonders from me. Like the new tricks of a star dog or elephant at the circus. But it gets ever harder with age, even though there is the inevitable maturing of your voice and more technical control.'

'Yes, that's exactly how I feel about my field and my work too.'

'And then there's Rita. She need its all, the fame and the status and the money. And now she's begun complaining about the pollution and bad infrastructure in India. She wants the superstar status we have in India. But the life and comforts of the US. I really do wonder now what I ever saw in her! Maybe, it was just my mother's machinations.'

'You said things weren't going well between you. What's up, *bhai*?'

'I think we're just too different. I find her shallow and materialistic, and she thinks I'm just an otherworldly loser.'

'And I suppose discussing it hasn't helped?'

'If only we could get to that stage. It usually just becomes an argument or a series of accusations. We're just totally incompatible. As it is, all she talks about is money.'

'And how about things at the school?'

'More of the same. I'm still a star. I suppose my reputation helps. But I don't play Madan's games, all these newfangled crowd-pleasing antics. And he's determined to push Niloy to centre-stage at all the school events and me to the sidelines.'

'And he doesn't listen to Guruji or your mother or Idanbai?'

'He pretends to. He's a pretty clever customer, this Cyrus Madan. He's all "Yes, yes, Guruji or Idanbaiji" to their faces. But in actual fact he's outlawed the use of *paan-daans* or *pik-daans* at the school. And he wants to trash Guruji's old spool recorder and gramophone, although he's still holding off on that. They're pretty eye-catching symbols in the school reception area you know. And also to remove the posters of the old masters in there and the main concert room. In fact, remove anything left over from the old *gharana* system really.'

'But surely he understands the need for some continuity and tradition. And that these do have some value in the market.'

'Well, I'm not so sure of that,' Nazrul says with a sigh. 'As it is, all he seems to talk of are either marketing gimmicks or the need for fancy new transducers and other state-of-the-art electronics for the fusion music he's forever pushing.'

'And what of Rita?' I ask.

'Oh, that's another thing Rita blames me for. Not playing Madan's games. She thinks they're necessary in today's world. I do wonder sometimes why people even want to marry. You know this, this eternal dance of the sexes.'

He suddenly bursts out laughing -- a harsh, ironic rasp, nothing like his usual chuckle. In spite of myself, something compels me to join in. Through the door, Lopa and Rita, who are stretched out side-by-side on the family room divan, turn to look at us.

'You probably don't know that Guruji had a stroke two days ago, Aniket. Do you?' Nazrul asks me.

I sit up bolt upright as though somebody has suddenly punctured my lungs. 'What! How is he?'

'He's partly paralysed and still in a coma. It happened after I talked to you day before yesterday from Montreal. I didn't have time to tell you at the airport or before the concert.'

'Let's go outside, Nazrul. I need some fresh air.'

2.7

About half an hour later we have congregated again in the living room. The fire has drawn us all back like a magnet.

'You don't actually go folk-dancing, do you, Aniket?' Rita asks. 'You had five left feet on the dance floor back in the old days.'

'Oh, yes, I do. And regularly at that. People can learn things, you know. I also go hiking and fishing. Can you imagine the old-time big-city Calcutta couch potato that I was even going near such things?'

'I wish I'd been a man. Then I could have had all the children I wanted and still been a famous singer,' Rita says with one of those abrupt transpositions that mark her conversations.

'How many would you have had?' Lopa asks softly.

'Oh, several! Except I don't know if I'd have the patience to bring them up.'

'Maybe it's just as well that you didn't have them then. You're famous and you have a famous husband as well. You're a star couple. Everybody talks about you,' Lopa says. 'You're very lucky in that way.'

'Want to trade places with me?' Rita says. 'Except I can't see myself teaching full-time, trying to beat donkeys into horses. Or living in a town like Lucknow, beautiful and cultured though it is. I need to be in one of the metros. But you chose the life you lead, didn't you, Lopa?'

'Yes, perhaps,' Lopa replies quietly. 'But can we really choose with so many restrictions and pressures all around? I had this peculiar dream around the time Ammi fell sick.'

'What about?' Nazrul says. 'I don't remember you ever mentioning it before.'

'Oh, it was like I was in a very large mansion with many floors. I lived there, and yet I didn't know many of the floors. I was choking, suffocating. And I began wandering around holding my throat, coughing, desperately seeking relief. And, as I came to the ground floor, a door to a basement – which I hadn't even known existed – suddenly opened up.'

'And?' Nazrul asks.

'As I went through it, I had this sense of panic, of something unknown and exciting but frightening nonetheless. There were strange doors to some of the rooms. I entered one of the rooms and a wild boar suddenly came charging out. But rather than gore me, it lifted me up on its back and tore out of one of the open doors. And suddenly the sense of choking was gone.'

'And that was all?' I say.

'No. Suddenly a lady wrapped in a white sari and carrying a *veena* was decorating my hair with some fragrant milk-white flowers which I couldn't identify. And she was smiling at me. And at that point I woke up.'

'I think you were feeling suffocated by your life in Lucknow. Perhaps Idanbai's illness even brought it to a head,' Nazrul says thoughtfully. 'And the boar was your hidden subconscious urge to break out. The lady in white is your muse, Lopa, the goddess Saraswati, the one you must follow.' I stare at him, my mouth falling slightly open. I had never known him to be an analyst of dreams.

'Do you remember the rehearsals for the festival at the school four years ago, Rita?' Lopa says, abruptly switching the conversation in a vein similar to Rita's.

'Yes, what of it?' says Rita.

'D'you remember that Guruji asked me to move to Calcutta and teach at the school? *Ammi* was beginning to be really sick around then, and it would have meant so much to us to be able to be together. She could have maintained her singing and it would have been a breath of fresh air for me. Even given the work of taking care of her, it would be a new beginning.'

'What of it?' Rita is suddenly guarded.

'Well, between you and Mr. Madan, you put paid to that. I still remember how you played the prima donna during the last day of the festival that year.'

'And you resent that,' Rita hisses. 'Not everyone can be a prima donna.'

Just as Lopa opens her mouth to utter a retort, Nazrul cuts in to break the tension. 'But no one's a prima donna forever either. Just look at my *Ammi*.'

'What d'you mean, Nazrul?' Rita snaps.

'She lives in her past now. Surrounded by pictures of herself as a star. She teaches when she's fit enough. But she's still trapped in the past – when she was the great Sureshwari

Devi, *ghazal* queen of India for so many decades. People cried over her singing. Thousands of young lovers sent cassettes of her songs, bundled in rose bouquets, to their beloved ones. Every VIP in the country feted and honoured her and invited her into their homes. It's all she can talk of.'

'But that's just how life is, Nazrul,' Rita says with a huff.

'But that's not really what I was getting at,' Lopa says hesitantly. 'I just needed a new beginning, and…'

'And I needed to move over and play dead?' Rita says icily.

'But I didn't want you to move over, Rita. I just needed to be given a position at the school, not to be a star.'

'Only over my dead body!'

'All right, all right,' Nazrul cuts in hurriedly. 'Let's talk of something else.'

'Perhaps we should turn in,' I say. 'It's been a long day. We're all just very tired. Tomorrow will be a new beginning.'

2.8

The waves are crashing onto the shoreline. And in the background is the black, hulking silhouette of a large mountain. It is still and dark like the Arunachala of legend.

In the foreground a figure is approaching. As he comes closer, I recognise him with a start. It is my *Dadu*. And now the waves part and something begins to rise to the surface. It is my *tanpura*. But it has been polished and is gleaming like new. As the waves crash into it, the strings come to life, sounding out an insistent refrain. And then *Dadu* reaches for it and he strums the refrain into a strange, hypnotic crescendo. It strikes my ears and careens up into my brain. And then it begins to resonate in my backbone, bouncing back and forth from the base of my spine to the point between my eyes. I cannot bear it. It is as if my head will explode into a thousand pieces. But *Dadu* does not stop. Does he want my head to shatter? I don't know how long it continues. But I cannot take it anymore. I pass out.

When I come to, the ringing in my head and spine have died away. There is no sign of either *Dadu* or the *tanpura*. The water has turned into a white ocean of milk. It stretches as far as my eye can see. The waves are white and there are bubbles and some movement.

Then, the waves part and a beautiful woman comes forth. She has a golden body and light radiates from it. Her body turns into molten gold and the radiance spreads to the surrounding waves. And then a huge lotus flower emerges from the depths with a golden tiara on it. And the woman places the crown on her head with a smile and takes her seat on the flower.

And now a radiant square plate made of some shining white metal arises from the waves. It it etched with a complicated concatenation of triangles of different sizes, all enclosed in circles. Shapes resembling the leaves of a lotus adorn the area between the circles. The whole figure is inscribed in a square. And now a new ringing sound arises from it and enters the spot between my eyes.

I awake with a start.

2.9

It is later that night. I have come downstairs to have my customary midnight snack. I am sitting at the kitchen dinette with a sandwich and a shot of brandy – small snifters are often the only things that knock me to sleep nowadays. Nazrul, a habitual late-night owl, is still up. He is sitting beside me, humming *Ka karoon sajni, aaye na baalam*.

'You know what I want to hear?' I say.

'What?'

'The song we grew up, and fell in love to. The immortal *thumri*...'

'You're pretty high, Aniket,' Nazrul says. 'I don't remember you this way before. Are you sure you should drink anymore?' Even in my present state, I can detect concern in his voice.

'It's all that's left, Nazrul. The only thing that dulls the pain. The true elixir of life. But let's sing, Nazrul.'

Just as we are about to start, there are footsteps in the living area. We turn to see Lopa framed in the doorway. She appears to hesitate and then advances towards us.

'Hi, both of you are still up?' she says uncertainly.

'Just a late-night snack. And a drink to wash it down with,' I reply. 'Want something?'

'No, thanks. But I'll join you.' She sits down at the tableand looks towards Nazrul. And then her eyes scan my face.

As I reach for the glass, Nazrul says, 'I've been trying to tell him to lay off the liquor. I think he's high enough.'

'It's my life. And my poison of choice.'

'Please, Aniket,' Lopa says. 'He's right. We've never seen you like this. Guruji hinted at something like this. And even Rita commented on it to me tonight.'

'Thanks, but no thanks. Why should you care? Now, Nazrul, his concern I can understand.'

'I can understand how you feel. But we're not free agents, Aniket.'

'You understand how I feel. How very empathetic of you,' I say with a sneer. 'Do you even remember how things were? How they might have been?'

'But it never could have worked, Aniket. We discussed this so many times.'

'You thought it couldn't work. And your mother was scared of every shadow and every dog she ever saw barking from any corner of the world of Indian classical music. Her world. That's all she knew. Or thought about. But that's changing. It wasn't really my world anyway. I was just a gatecrasher. The upstart who thought he could sing. Who gave up at the first obstacle? And now you see what happens to parvenu gatecrashers. They have their heads sheared and spend their days in sackcloth and ashes.' I take a large swig of brandy.

After a long pause, Lopa says, 'Can I tell you a story, Aniket? In principle, it's a story you know. But I'm not sure that you ever really understood.'

'Will it make me understand? The penny will finally drop. The blockhead will see the light.'

'Oh, how does it even matter? How does anything matter? What's the point of even talking anyway!' Lopa exclaims.

'Exactly. But tell me anyway,' I growl. 'You always did like stories, especially fairy tales.'

'Well, it's a story about a girl who never knew her father. And her mother, the most wonderful, kind person in the world. She saw her mother abused and even insulted for being a *baiji*. Ever since, she was a little girl, that was their reality. It was rarely to their face, for her mother had begun to become famous by virtue of her incredible musical talent. But it always hung over them. Everything she ever learnt and everything she ever became was because of this wonderful mother. But this shadow hung over them and over her ever since her childhood. It coloured everything, even her earliest memories.'

'Well, a very touching story. One I already know, as you said. Would make a great Hindi movie. But it doesn't tug at my heartstrings.'

There is a long silence. Then Lopa says, 'But can't you understand? Can't you see? I couldn't go against her wishes.'

'Well, that was clear enough. I guess I should really thank my stars, shouldn't I? What a paragon of virtue she is, I should tell myself every day. How loyal she was to her mother! Tell me, how does it feel to destroy a life? But that's beside the point, I suppose.'

I regret the last words even as they came out of some dark corner of my mind. Even in my drunk state, I regret saying them. Lopa turns ashen and walks off without another word.

2.10

'Come here, Tom,' Prem says to his student who has arrived in Ithaca early the following morning. Prem has planted himself firmly mid-stream in the pool of water about a hundred feet away from the base of the massive drop of the Taughannock Falls outside Ithaca. The snowstorm has finally lifted and there are even hints of sunshine peeping out from behind the clouds. The trip to Taughannock has been planned ahead of time and Ithaca's notoriously fickle winter weather seems to be cooperating.

Tom advances gingerly into the puddle next to Prem. I am unsure of what Prem has up his sleeve. Even knowing him as I do, I am taken aback by what happens next. They stand in mid-stream and start singing loudly, circling round and round and gyrating their hips in contortions that would test any professional *Bhangra* dancer.

'So this is what Madan wants to import into our school, courtesy this buffoon,' Nazrul says snarkily.

****

Half an hour later, we are ensconced in the Indian eatery Kohinoor. Prem appears to still be in the somewhat manic mood he has displayed at the Falls. As we order, he suddenly tells the waitress. 'I want two gallons of milk and all the *jalebis* you have in the restaurant.'

'What're you up to, Prem?' Nazrul asks.

'You know the ustads of old, *yaar*, like Ustad Haddu Khan. This was their ideal breakfast.'

'It was the traditional breakfast in north India in the old days,' I say. 'But why this sudden urge on your part?'

'I'm feeling high, *yaar*. It's just the effect of seeing all you old friends after all these years. You know that Haddu Khan would do two hundred and fifty don *baithaks*, push-ups, first thing in the morning. And then bathe in water drawn from a well.'

'I suppose the spectacle you put up at the Falls was your modern equivalent?' Nazrul says drily.

'And then he'd follow it up with a breakfast of fifty *jalebis* dropped into a bucket containing two *seers* of milk. Milk's good for the throat,' he adds, ignoring Nazrul.

'He also followed that up with four hours of practice of his deadly *gamak* and *halak taans*' Nazrul says. 'They made the windows of the nearby *imambara* rattle. I hope you're not hoping to similarly regale us during our rehearsal.'

'I'll do my best, *yaar*,' Prem says with his characteristic good humour. 'He was a great man. D'you know that he once went to visit the Taj Mahal with Faiyaz Khan's grandfather Gulam Abbas Khan? On seeing it, his reaction was, "What's so great about this cupola, it's just the equivalent of one note of my *taans*."'

'He certainly was a great singer,' Lopa says. 'His *taans* were magnificent. *Ammi* says that in those days, they had names for *taans* such as *kadak bijli* or flashing lightning *taan*, *nanga talwar* or bared sword *taan*, and *hathi chinghaar* or elephant exciting *taan*.'

'I've never even heard of those,' Prem says. 'Were the names literally true?'

'My mother's heard eyewitness accounts that once Haddu Khan and his brother Hassu Khan performed the deadly *hathi chinghaar taan,* which had been known to actually incite elephants to stampede from their quarters in the *pilkhana,* at the court of the Maharaja of Gwalior.'

'And seeing this, Ustad Bare Mubarak Ali's father, the famed Mohammed Khan had cried out "Subhan Allah, Subhan Allah!" in astonishment.' I say. 'And then he asked that they repeat the *taan* which, on other occasions, had even cracked the charpoy they were sitting on down the middle. It was one of Guruji and my *Dadu's* favourite stories,' I add as an afterthought.

'Yes,' Lopa says. 'But when they attempted to repeat it, blood gushed out from Ustad Hassu Khan's mouth.'

'You sure that's not just a tall tale?' Prem drawls.

'Well, the story's not over. The eyewitness accounts say that his grandfather, Ustad Natthan Pir Baksh was present there. And he walked up to his grandson and wiped the blood from his mouth with his own shawl. And then he said, "*Beta, marna hi hai to taan puri karke maro. Khaandaan ka izzat ka sawaal hai.*" "Son, if you must die, then do so after completing the *taan.* It's a matter of our family honour."'

'Just BS, plain and simple,' Prem yawns. 'We Indians are really full of it.'

'Well, maybe,' says Nazrul. 'But we'll be expecting the real-life equivalent from you.'

Mr. Madan, who has been indulgently watching the proceedings, now butts in, 'On that note ladies and gentlemen, I suggest that we head back for the rehearsal.'

2.11

Keiko Yajima watches as Rita tunes her *tanpura* carefully. Nearby, Mr. Madan observes Nazrul doing his warm-up exercises for the throat.

Nazrul repeatedly hits the tonic or *shadaja* of the ultra-low register with the use of a full-throated, open-lipped *aah* or *aakaar* sound in the time-honoured way. Tradition has it that this is the key to the mystical realms of vocal music. It is a practice closely linked to the meditative and monastic Hindu and Sufi practice of toning the *chakras* or energy centres along the spine using vowel sounds, and overtoning using *mantras* or combinations of vowels and consonants.

As Nazrul finishes and moves on to a stunning web of *taans*, I am drawn into the river of sound. I listen to him perform the *bahalwa,* combining *mirs* – glissandos – with *laraj* for the next ten minutes. He stays below the *gandhar* or mi all the while and yet never repeats a sequence as he moves smoothly from one permutation to the next.

He has matured into everything he promised to be. The years of *riyaz* have brought *taasir,* an ocean of overtones. His voice is now hypnotically resonant and audible even at the lowest volumes and frequencies. But more than that is the sense of *swar-siddhi,* a sense of musical attainment, the sort of perfection a listener feels but cannot really put into words.

'Some more pep, Nazrul!' Mr. Madan barks, putting paid to my thoughts in no uncertain fashion. 'A modern audience can't stand this for very long. Step on the gas. Some fireworks, please.'

My eyes fall on Lopa, sitting quietly in a corner.

The door opens and Prem Kishan enters with his American disciple Tom. 'Now you can have all the fireworks you want,' Nazrul says. His tone is polite and perfectly neutral, but the hint of steel is clear.

Mr. Madan frowns exasperatedly. 'At least Prem Kishan's established himself here. I'm sure you'll agree that he can teach us many tricks of the trade about how to sell our music to a modern audience, Nazrul.'

'Can't you think of anything else besides selling, Cyrus? We're not hawking underwear or soap you know!'

'Well, we'd better pretend as though we are, or we'll be out of business before you know it.' Mr. Madan says as he hastens forward to greet Prem. 'You're just not willing to deal with reality, Nazrul. Take off your rose-tinted glasses. Smell the coffee.'

Prem Kishan begins bustling around in his usual hearty manner. He clowns a bit with Tom. *'Mera chai ka pyala,'* they trill, and then 'My cows they are a- a- grazing.'

'What on earth is that?' I ask.

'A recent hit,' says Prem. 'It's what sells in the States. And the second one's composed by Ravi Shang-kaar and sung by Lakshmi Shang-kaar, you know!'

'Really smelly coffee,' I hear Nazrul mutter.

A few minutes later the door opens again and some NRIs from Syracuse and Elmira enter. Not the greatest of classical music aficionados. I consider warning Nazrul and Lopa to not get too deep in conversation with them. Some of these NRI doctors and engineers become know-it-all pseudo-intellectuals once they have their single-family homes with two cars, the gigantic theatre system in the living room, bone china in the kitchen cabinets and all the latest electronic gizmos all around. The dollars-in-the-ghetto effect.

After the introductions are done and Mr. Madan has introduced Prem as the great star of Indian classical music in New York City, there is much ooh-ing and aah-ing. I am reminded of a wisecrack an NRI friend once made on being asked whether he'd faced culture shock upon arriving in the US. 'Not from the Americans,' he said with a straight face. 'But when I met the NRI crowd, especially at cultural events. You know, middle-aged women stomping about on the stage like elephants. Or everyone offstage enjoying their food and drink and *gup-shup* while adults freely and proudly sing totally off-key, but onstage. Now THAT was a real culture shock.'

'So just how did you make it here?' one of the newcomers asks Prem.

'It was initially quite a struggle,' Prem replies. 'I gave some lessons. You know, there was already some interest in Indian classical music by the time I arrived. And I gave some concerts in Greenwich Village and Soho to the discerning few and to some New Age composers and enthusiasts.'

'And after that?' Mr. Madan asks, clearly hanging on to every word that falls from the lips of this great master of selling Indian classical music to new audiences.

'Well, I tried *raga* therapy for common diseases for a while. Again it did well for some time in the counter-culture circuit and among some of the upper class New Yorkers who'd already heard about meditation and yoga and tai chi and the like.'

'So what exactly did you do?' asks one of the NRIs.

'Well,' Prem smirks, 'I'd read about how Pandit Onkarnath Thakur used to advocate different *ragas* for treating different diseases. So we came up with a tonoscope, a machine that you placed on a person's sternum to identify their basic tone or *shadaja*. And then, based on that, I prescribed the *ragas* I'd read up about for various ailments.'

Nazrul almost doubles up with laughter in the background. Certainly the idea of a suffering New Yorker, perhaps one of the ubiquitous hippies who surround Prem, crumpled up, while our friend vibrates a tuning fork off his body like our high-school experiments in sound makes for a very colourful mental picture.

'That would be great therapy,' says one of the NRIs, his thick Malayalee accent still audible behind a painfully contrived nasal New York twang. Mr. Madan adds his assent with a vigorous shake of his head.

'I love guzzles,' a teenager accompanying one of the NRIs says innocently, bringing immediate smiles to our faces.

The next minute, they are wiped off as another NRI chimes in, 'I would love to invite you to my house for tomorrow evening. I sing too, you know.'

For once, even Mr. Madan and Prem Kishan are at a loss for words. But the man seems oblivious. 'I'll sing for you,' he continues. 'Film songs, you know?'

Prem Kishan seems to have found his voice. 'Songs related to classical *thumris* or *dadras*?' he asks.

'*Dadra*? What's that? No, no, just film songs,' the NRI replies blithely.

Nazrul whispers to me, 'Holy smokes. D'you think he really means it?'

'Oh yes,' I say. 'I didn't realise it when I first got here, but the dollar salary seems to give some NRIs the license to be oracles and experts on everything under the sun. And their Bollywood guests seem to humour them. Maybe they don't know any better.'

'Oracles on everything from aalpin to elephant, or a pin to an elephant, as Utpal Dutt's character says in Ray's *Jana Aranya*,' Nazrul chuckles.

'You hit that pin right on the head.'

2.12

'The news isn't good,' says Nazrul, hanging up the phone. 'It doesn't look like

Guruji will make it through the day.'

Cyrus Madan, Nazrul and I are having an after-dinner liqueur on the patio. As on the previous day, the evening concert has gone off extremely well. Prem Kishan and Tom are already on their way back to New York City. Lopa and Rita, perhaps motivated by the events of the previous evening, have accepted an invitation to spend the night at Michael and Keiko's place.

'You must come to Calcutta this year, Aniket *babu*,' Mr. Madan says in his usual hearty manner. 'We will definitely organise a festival in memory of Guruji.'

'When are you planning to hold it?' I say. 'Anyway, he's not gone yet.'

'I know that you can only come during the summer months when you usually visit us. Perhaps, July will be a good time. The monsoons will have set in good and proper by then, so it won't be as hot. We will make sure that you're there. But maybe we can do it during the annual music festival in December.'

'Of course I'd come. It would be the least I could do to honour Guruji's memory.'

'That settles that then. It's been a long day, so I will turn in, if you don't mind,' Mr. Madan says.

After settling him in his bedroom, Nazrul and I return to the living area. 'You must come for an extended visit this time, Aniket. Not just for the festival Cyrus mentioned,' he says, as we settle down on the sofa beside the fireplace.

'Why, Nazrul, is there any particular reason?' I ask, pretending to not understand.

'I think we – all three of us, you, Lopa and me – we're at a time of reckoning, *bhai*. Remember what the *Baul*, the *sadhu* or *pir*, whatever you call him, told us those many years ago in Shantiniketan?'

Of course I remember. 'It would be fun to go to the *baul* haunts again. After all these years. Of course you've been going there off and on anyway.'

'I'll tell you some stories about some initiations I've received. But I'll need to take permission first.'

'That'd be great. I'll need to check how long I can come down for,' I say with caution.

'Stop playing games, *bhai*. You know you want to come and need to come. Remember Mr. Bellety stirringly elocuting Mark Anthony's speech in Julius Caeser, "There comes a time in the affairs of men, which, taken at the flood..."'

'But d'you see any flood cresting in my life? I see only an ebb-tide, ebbing out and away, ever further.'

Nazrul is silent for what seems like an eternity as we sip our brandies. Then he says, 'I think that one's coming, Aniket – I mean a flood. I'm wondering what, if anything, I should tell you though?'

'Now that sounds really mysterious. Like some oracle speaking in riddles.'

'Let me tell you this much, *bhai*. Make of it what you want. Lopa told me today that she couldn't sleep most of last night after your encounter in the kitchen. And then, when she fell fitfully to sleep, she dreamt that she was drowning and suffocating when suddenly a man appeared beside her. And he was preparing to put a ring on her finger.'

'And?'

'She resisted, and stretched out the ring finger on her right hand very stiffly. And then she awoke in a cold sweat.'

I try to sound casual, but I know that Nazrul, of all people, certainly senses how I am quivering inside. 'But what does that have to do with me, Nazrul? After last night? After all the water that's flowed under the bridge?'

'I told you, *bhai*. Draw your own conclusions. But I think you will spend an interesting summer in Calcutta.' He gently places his hand on my forearm as he says this.

We sit for some more minutes, each sunk in our own thoughts. Then, with the silent understanding that only decades of friendship and years of singing together can bring, we stand up, exchange a long embrace and head to our bedrooms.

2.13

The ocean of milk again. Its surface is turbulent with violent waves and vortices. There is no parting of the surface this time, just a continuous churning motion that makes me faintly queasy. And then I see the hulking silhouette of the dark mountain in the background and I am desperately trying to clamber up its slopes. But with each step I take, I fall back.

And now, as before, a figure appears in the foreground. It is *Dadu*. He holds me by the hand and gently and effortlessly leads me up the slope to the summit.

To my surprise, I see a reclining figure spread-eagled on a multihued *dhuree* rug. *Dadu* leads me forward and points to the face. With a shudder, I see that it is me. I reach forward. The figure is icy cold to the touch. I look up. *Dadu* is smiling down at me kindly. 'Yes, *Dadubhai*,' he whispers. 'It is you.'

'But why, *Dadu*? Why?'

He does not answer. He only looks at me with a mixture of compassion and sadness.

And now the waves are parting. I half expect to see my *tanpura* or the golden goddess from before. But this time, it is Guruji holding the metal plate with the mystical symbols from before. He walks straight towards me. When he is about two feet away, he says, "I'm going, *beta*. But my blessings will always be with you. Always remember me." Then he turns the metal plate towards me. I feel the light from it strike the spot between my eyes. It enters and I am suddenly dizzy.

As I pass out, I dimly hear Guruji's voice tracing the path taken by the light, echoing in my brain at first and then careening down my spine, 'Come, Ashutosh-*dada*. It is time.'

****

When I come to, I am curled up, in near-foetal position. But surprisingly, I have a feeling of strength, almost of rejuvenation.

I step out of bed into my slippers, slip on my dressing gown and walk over to Nazrul's bedroom. I shake him awake. 'Nazrul, Nazrul, I think that Guruji is no more. I KNOW that he's gone.....'

'It's an unearthly, ungodly hour, Aniket! How d'you know? How can you be sure?' He rubs his eyes sleepily.

'He came to me in a dream to say goodbye. Oh Nazrul, soon Idanbai will be gone as well! The world we knew will have vanished for good.'

ASTHAYI (COMPOSITION)

Lucknow, Calcutta and Kanpur, 1957-1974

My days didn't remain confined to their golden cage,

Those rainbow-hued days of mine.

They didn't hold

Those bonds of laughter and of tears,

Of those many-splendoured days of mine.

I had hopes that they would learn

The language of the song of my soul

But they flew off

Without telling any of their tales,

Those rainbow-hued days of mine.

Now I dream that the stars come,

And circle around the broken cage

Of those many-splendoured days of mine.

– Rabindranath Tagore

3.1

It is 1957 in Lucknow. My music-loving – perhaps music-infatuated is more accurate – *Dadu* or grandfather, Ashutosh Mukherjee, is a leading lawyer of the city's High Court. Today he has dragged Pandit Vishnu Joshi – a professor at Lucknow's famous Marris College of Music, later to become my music teacher and beloved Guruji – and my reluctant self to a leaf hut on the city's outskirts. As we enter I hear him tell Guruji, 'Vishnu, please keep a watch over me. If I become unbalanced, just tug on my shirt.'

The aged Ustad, the son of Chote Munne Khan, the last surviving singer of Nawab Wajid Ali Shah's famous musical durbars before his deposition by the British, seems agitated. 'Where will I seat you, Mukherjee *saab* and Pandit Joshiji?' he asks.

They smile and reply, '*Koi baat nahi, Ustad. Koi baat nahi. Is chote mote baat ki phikar na kijiye.*' ('No matter, Ustad. No matter. Don't worry about such a triviality.') We take our seats on the tattered ropes strung across the frame of the old *charpoy*. It creaks and shifts ominously but holds. Some more pleasantries are followed by *Dadu* saying, 'A *Bhairavi thumri*, Ustad. And then perhaps a *bara khayal*.' Then the singing begins.

To my six-year-old ears, it seems interminable. Incomprehensible sequences of sound, sometimes slow and dragging, and like bursts of artillery fire at others. After some time, I scamper over to the second *charpoy* at the far end of the room, yawn and curl up into a ball.

The next thing I know, *Dadu* is shaking me awake. '*Khokone, beta, chol. Jabar shomoi hoeche.*' ('*Khokone*, son, come. It's time to go.') Through the window, I see that the sun is high in the sky. We have been here for at least three hours.

As we leave the hut, *Dadu* presses several notes into the Ustad's son's hands. Then, before our *tonga* leaves, in the courteous Lucknavi style, he tells the Ustad and his son, '*Janaab, kisi roz hamaare gareeb-khane pe tashrif rakkhiye-ga.*' ('Sirs, please grace my humble abode with your presence someday.') They all smile. Some more waves and we are off.

After some time, Guruji tells *Dadu*, 'You will come this evening, won't you? We've just received some rare old 78 rpm records of old masters. I'm sure you'd love to listen to them.'

Dadu smiles and nods. 'Yes, of course Vishnu. It will be a delight, I'm sure.'

'Can I come? Can I come?' I ask, tugging at *Dadu's* sleeve.

He looks at me with his usual indulgent smile. 'Yes, your *Dida* doesn't feel well today, so you can't stay with her,' he says, referring to my grandmother. 'But you mustn't fidget. We'll be listening to music again.'

'I promise. Cross my heart,' I say, proudly mouthing this recently-learned phrase.

'Maybe he can bring some toys along? They'll keep him occupied,' Guruji suggests. 'I realise that he can't stay at home since his parents…' He breaks off, biting his lip. Like other adults, he doesn't want to mention my parents who have been killed in a car crash in Simla the previous year.

'He's getting to be quite a reader,' *Dadu* says. '*Khokone*, why don't you bring along your *Thakurmar Jhuli* and the latest issue of *Sandesh*?' As I bounce around delightedly, he explains to Guruji, 'That's a collection of ghost stories and a famous Bengali children's magazine published from Calcutta.'

3.2

It is about three years later, sometime during the winter of 1960. Guruji, Dadu and I are in the larger rehearsal-cum-performance room of Marris College. Along the walls are posters of past music conferences and old masters. Occupying pride of place in the centre is a large poster from the famous Grand Conference organised by the legendary singer and musicologist Pandit Bhatkhande in Lucknow's Kaiserbagh Baradari in 1925.

In one corner is a large gramophone. And next to it is a tall statue of a dog with the words 'His Master's Voice' emblazoned across it. It will be some years before I realise that the dog is from some past promotional campaign run by the Gramophone Company of India.

I see a glint of metal in a corner of the room and walk over. Guruji is sifting through a small pile of pins, looking for a clean, rust-free one. He finds one and slips it into the hole in the gramophone's curved metal tone-arm. Then he looks up and shouts across the room to *Dadu*, 'Ashutosh *dada*, what should we start with?'

'Abdul Karim Khan,' *Dadu* declares. 'I've heard so much about him.'

'Abdul Karim Khan it is. Let's start with *Jamuna ke teer*. But where're your visitors?'

'Let's start without them,' *Dadu* says. 'Sureshwari Devi has brought along a holy man from Calcutta. She introduced him as Tyaagi Baba, the renunciate *baba*. I couldn't tell whether he's a Muslim *pir* or a Hindu *sadhu*. I think they'll come when this *baba* wakes up. He was taking a nap when we left.'

'Oh yes! I saw him smoking something before that,' I offer. 'It was like a long clay pipe. He lit it with a piece of rope and then he was puffing away through the holes in the side.'

'He certainly notices everything,' Guruji smiles.

'What was it, *Dadu*? What was he smoking?'

'The pipe is called a *chillum, Khokone*. I'll tell you about it when you grow up.

You know how curiosity killed the cat. Be a good boy now, will you? Go and read quietly in the corner while we listen.'

3.3

It is 1962. India and China are at war. I have seen fighter jets in the sky several days in a row. All the boys in school have been talking excitedly about the planes used in the Second World War, the Stukas and the Hunters, the Spitfires and Meschersmitts and the Japanese Zeros. How camouflage improved by leaps and bounds during the war and the development of radar and the jet engine. As we walked back from school one day, we saw a convoy of tanks and armoured cars roll past us.

It is a Sunday, so both my school and *Dadu's* court are shut. We are about to visit Guruji at Marris College this morning when one of the *rickshawallas* whom *Dida* has allowed to stay in the spare garage comes rushing up the stairs.

'What is it, Ramu?' *Dadu* asks the panting man.

'*Saab*, the cow we were keeping for milk seems to have gone mad. You must come immediately. She's charging round and round in circles in the garage.

Gonra and Mahadev tried to stop him. He's gored Gonra in the right leg, *saab*.'

'You go on ahead to the College then, *Khokone*,' *Dadu* says. 'Vishnu will be waiting for us. But this sounds serious. Tell him what's happened and that I'll join you as soon as I can. Ramu, please take him in the rickshaw, will you?'

About an hour later, I am sitting next to the gramophone in the Marris College music room humming softly to myself.

'Oh, you're singing Moujdin's famous *dadra* '*Nadiya nare hirai aayi kangana*', *beta*,' Guruji's voice startles me out of my reverie. 'Do you know that he was self-taught? Actually, he would pick up any piece or movement, no matter how complex, after hearing it once.'

'Yes, Vishnu uncle. I've heard the story of his musical genius from *Dadu*. He called it an eidetic musical memory, together with an inborn *swar-siddhi*.'

'Yes, it was as though he was born with all of the musical attainment that the greatest musicians strive for all their lives and only very few attain. But you were singing the variations of the *mukhda* so effortlessly. I didn't know you had picked it up just by listening here. Let's play it and see.' Guruji steps towards the gramophone.

'Can I operate it? Please, Vishnu uncle! Please let me try it!'

'You're getting quite interested in music, I see,' Guruji says with a smile. 'I worry that you might scratch the records, *beta*. The pin has to be placed very gently at the outer edge. And some of these records are really collector's items. They're impossible to replace if they get scratched.'

'If they're so valuable, why doesn't HMV re-issue them? And why do the new ones have the same design on the jackets, just in different colours? Look at the old ones. How colourful and different the jackets were!'

Dadu walks in at this moment. '*Dadu*, can I operate the gramophone? Please, please let me, please. Tell Vishnu uncle to let me. Please, *Dadu*! I won't scratch the records. I promise.'

'D'you have some really old, scratched records Vishnu?' *Dadu* asks Guruji. When Guruji nods in the affirmative, he continues, 'Give me some. I'll give *Khokone* some old pins and let him practice with them on the scratched discs at home.'

'Yes, of course. But have you considered having him learn music? What d'you say to it, Aniket *beta*?'

I remain silent. *Dadu* asks, 'Why d'you say that, Vishnu?'

'I see that he's beginning to be interested. And I heard him hum under his breath. He carries complicated tunes quite effortlessly, it seems. He's your grandson, after all.'

'Will you take him on as your student, Vishnu?' *Dadu* says.

'I will if he wants to learn. He's eleven, isn't he? It'll be too late after this.'

Two hours later, we are walking home after another long session at the gramophone, listening to rare pieces by old masters. We turn into J.G. Carr and Company to buy our favourite flavours of English peppermints, and garters and straps for the checked knee-length plaid socks and *khaki* shorts which are Dadu's weekend attire.

As we wait in line at the cashier's, Dadu turns to me and asks, 'What d'you say about learning singing from Vishnu, *Khokone*? It would be the opportunity of a lifetime. People come from all over the country to learn from him.'

'I'm hungry now, *Dadu*,' I say instead. 'I'll have to think about it.'

'He said that you may have talent. That he caught you humming under your breath.'

'*Dadu*, you know what? I just discovered that I could carry a tune a few months back. Six months ago, I was convinced that I could sing only one song.

You know which one, right?'

'The national anthem,' *Dadu* replies.

3.4

There is a crowd of noisy children milling around the front gate of the La Martinere School for Boys. The girls are from the adjacent school. Rickshaws and cars are pulling up, disgorging children who melt into the melee waving to any family members who have come to drop them off. In the distance is the magnificent Indo-Moorish-Italianate structure of the old Constantia Building, now home to La Martinere College and a golf course, with its fluted columns and Moorish cupola or *laat*. Behind it, the waters of the Gomti River gleam through the gaps in the structure.

The school bell rings out, resonant and insistent. The boys and girls head for the separate gates of their schools. The class monitors and prefects line them up.

I rush forward to greet my friend Prashant. A little girl is tugging at his shirt.

'This is my little sister, Nandini,' Prashant says. 'She's refusing to go to her own class. This is only her second week in school and she wants to stay with me.'

'Maybe send her home with your *rickshawalla*,' I say. 'You know him well. He's reliable, isn't he?'

'How about it Nandini, d'you want to go home with Ram Sharan?' Prashant asks his sister in Hindi.

There is a swift, decisive shake of Nandini's little head which sends her pigtails flying.

'But what'll you do then?' Prashant asks, surprised.

'I'll go with you!'

As we are shepherded towards the classroom, we explain the situation to the prefect in charge. He smiles and lets us through.

Fifteen minutes later, our teacher, Mrs. Peterson, enters. Her hawk eye immediately settles on Nandini, sitting snuggled up to Prashant. 'Prashant, who's that with you?' she asks in her whip-like tone.

Explanations follow and then Mrs. Peterson advances towards Nandini. 'You can't stay here, *beti*,' she says, her voice surprisingly softer now. 'Let me take you to the Headmaster's office.' As she reaches for Nandini, the classroom is rent by a loud shriek, 'Ooh, ooh!' followed by a giggle from Nandini and the cry, 'She's bitten me! Laugh, will you, you little wench!'

Pandemonium breaks out in the room. Teachers from the adjoining classrooms begin to peep in. Shortly afterwards, the classrooms lining our corridor are treated to the spectacle of Nandini being half carried and half frog-marched down to the main office. Prashant trails along, trying in vain to reason with her.

Much to our delight, Mrs. Peterson seems to have disappeared together with the offender. We are warned repeatedly about rowdiness for the rest of the hour.

Later, the general science teacher, Mr. D'Sa, marches in for the next period wearing a mischievous smirk. Without a word and to our complete astonishment, he begins writing on the blackboard in his bold scrawl, 'Three quarts of rice flour, one quart of *tur daal* flour……'

Ten minutes later, he ends the recipe with a flourish, followed by the clincher 'The above gives a dosa. My name is D'SA!' The class erupts into renewed merriment.

It has been an eventful start to our day. But the surprises continue to pile up.

Shortly after the lunch break, a peon knocks on the classroom door. He confers with the teacher and then Prashant is called outside. He does not return.

When I see him two hours later, after the final bell dismissing the school, he is sitting with a worried look outside the main office. Nandini is missing.

After waiting for her for some time, I proceed with him to the rickshaws outside the main gate. Ram Sharan is squatting at his usual spot on the footpath next to a broken fire hydrant which serves as the regular water supply for the school's *churan* and *phuchkawalla*. He is rolling his *khaini* in his hands and chatting animatedly with the other *rickshawallas*.

As soon as he sees us, he points to me and bursts out, 'Saab, *bitiya* made me go to this *saab*'s house!' Our mouths fall open.

Half an hour later, we find the little brat Nandini ensconced in the small room adjacent to *Dadu's* office-cum-library. She is contentedly chomping away at a pile of peanuts while rolling the dice for a game of Ludo with *Dadu's munshiji*.

She doesn't even acknowledge our presence. Prashant gives her a slight slap on her back and in his best big brother tone says, 'You harassed us all day! First you were naughty in the class. And then, you didn't even say anything, but just vanished.'

'Why did they force me to leave you?' she says in between some more rolls of the dice.

'So why didn't you just go home? You know I was sick with worry! What would I have told our parents?' Prashant says patiently.

Munshiji intervenes, '*Jaane do, saab. Ro rahi thi jab ayee yahan pe. Itni dari hui thi ki khatiya ke neeche chupne-wali thi.*' ('Let it be, *saab*. She was crying when she arrived. She was so scared they'd drag her back that she wanted to hide under the bed.')

'Mama would have scolded me if I went home,' Nandini retorts. 'I had so much fun here all afternoon.'

We almost burst out laughing. *Munshiji* pats Nandini approvingly on the back. Even Prashant's irritation has given way to a smile. As for me, the song *Nanhe munne bacche, tere ankhon me kya hai* begins playing in my mind.

3.5

It is the last evening of the 1962 festival at the Marris College of Music. This is a much more elaborate affair than the regular college concerts for Ganesh Chaturthi, Saraswati Puja and the birthday of the school's founder, the legendary singer and musicologist Pandit Vishnu Narayan Bhatkhande. This annual *'Sangeet Dhara'* festival features three days and nights of continuous musical programmes.

All the guests are being welcomed with *attar*, floral garlands and glasses of *badaam sherbet*. As the principal of the college, Pandit Vishnu Joshi – formally my Guruji for the past few months – is to give the closing performance. And then an outdoor movie show will run through the rest of the night.

Since my entry into the school as a student, I have learnt that Guruji has developed a unique fusion of the styles of the two oldest *gharanas* of north Indian classical music, the Agra and Gwalior schools. Both are famous for their *raga vistaar*, and in Guruji's fusion they have assumed a dazzling variety. In this aspect, many agree that he has taken over the mantle of his guru, the previous principal of the College, the legendary Pandit Sri Krishna Ratanjankar.

Guruji steps onto the stage in a black silk *achkan* and matching Nehru cap to a burst of applause. When he steps off two hours later, he has bewitched us. His first piece, a *khayal* in *Raga Gopi Basant*, is a tour de force. But what follows is a display of extraordinary virtuosity and skill, as he strings five closely-related *ragas* of the same family, *ragas Purwa*, *Puriya*, *Purvi*, *Saanjh-giri* and *Sohini* together in sequence, presenting each with its distinct flavour, mood and rhythmic and tonal development. This is an achievement that would test the greatest singers.

As he finishes, he rises to his feet with folded hands. After the applause dies, he says, 'Friends, I have an announcement to make. It will sadden many of you, my loyal friends and students and fans here, to know that I have accepted a position at a music school in Calcutta. I will always miss this most beautiful among the Islamic cities of India which has given so much to north Indian music. All the modern forms of north Indian vocal music were pioneered in this state, and no one has learnt more or been enriched more musically by it than me. But it is time for new blood here. And it is time for me to move on to other things.'

There is a hushed silence in the crowd. Obviously, they have not suspected anything like this even in their wildest dreams.

I have known about this for some time. Indeed, I know from Guruji's discussions with Dadu that the decline of the Lucknow aristocracy has been one of the factors in his decision. 'Calcutta offers better prospects now,' I have heard him say.

An all-night screening of the films *Madhumati* and *Mughal-e-Azam* will follow. As the *pandal* is taken down for the show, the imposing remains of the Kaiserbagh complex come into view. It is hard to even imagine how magnificent it must have been in Wajid Ali Shah's time, before most of the major structures were systematically demolished by the

British. The single surviving structure, housing our school, has an ethereal majesty in the brilliant glow of the near full moon.

Normally obscured by the rush of traffic in the daytime, the ionic columns, the ornate banisters and Moorish minarets and the Hindu umbrellas with lanterns and pediments look like some magical fairy's palace in the dim light. The gigantic shadows cast by the two remaining *'Lakhi'* gates of the *Baradari* in the distance heighten the feeling as they reach forward towards us like ghostly witch's wings.

Everyone settles down on the grassy knoll to enjoy the show.

3.6

A mass of teeming children from the neighbourhood line the stairs leading to the terrace of our home. It is time for the Diwali fireworks. The neighbourhood is aglow with the *diyas* adorning the windows and grills of all the homes.

On the street below, an irate mother is dragging along a reluctant child. I hear snippets of the heated exchange drifting up to our rooftop perch. 'Bunk school, and think that you'll fool us, will you! How many times have I warned you? If it happens again or you get a bad report card, I swear that you'll never hear the last of it! You'll go with us today and every other day. Those loafer friends of yours and their fireworks can wait.'

Next to them, another group of boys seem intent on completing their kill of a couple of caterpillars hanging from the underside of a leaf. They have been at it for at least fifteen minutes, hunting the creatures down systematically leaf by leaf, branch by branch. It is a difficult business in the fast-gathering gloom.

A couple of the boys from the neighbouring house and I have been flying kites for the past two hours. But now our last two surviving kites, the only ones left from the tangles with others being flown from the neighbourhood roofs, are nearly in tatters. We rush inside to *Dadu's* office. He is still not home from his Saturday evening drive. *Munshiji* is sitting in his bedroom, adjoining the office, poring over some legal papers.

'*Munshiji*,' I say, 'Give us some money, please, for some kites. *Ghuddi ke liye kuch paisa de dijiye.'*

He looks up and breaks into a smile as one of my friends adds, 'It's Diwali. Treat us to some sweets as well.'

Before he can reply, there is a commotion outside the doorway leading out from the stairwell onto the terrace. This is followed by a sequence of ear-splitting explosions punctuated by screams and cries. And then some girls come running helter-skelter out onto the roof.

The explosions do not cease. As we rush into the stairwell to investigate, they continue to rumble, growing fainter and receding downwards towards the lower floors. As I exchange glances with two other boys, I notice a sudden blaze on the first floor. The acrid smell of smoke comes floating up together with the glow from leaping sparks down below. 'Oh no!' I yell. 'It's my 78s! They were piled up beneath the stairs. They've caught fire.'

Half an hour later, after the flames have been doused with buckets of water, the cause is still hard to identify. 'Someone must've set off fireworks in the stairwell without realising how dangerous they can be in a closed space. Luckily, nothing serious happened. But let this be a lesson to all of you,' *Dadu* tells us. He has just returned from his outing.

Suddenly *Munshiji* emerges onto the landing near the charred 78 rpm records where we are gathered. He is dragging *Didi*, my older sister behind him. '*Saab, bitiya* did it. She had a string of small fireworks and she threw them up into the stairwell.'

'But why, *Munshiji*?' *Dadu* asks. 'She didn't understand what could happen. Is that why?'

Didi answers, 'He said that I was bad. And then, I threw his shoe out of the window.'

Munshiji scowls and continues, 'It fell on the head of a lady passing below. And she came charging in. So I had to scold *bitiya*.'

'Yes, of course,' says *Dadu*. 'I'm too old to really discipline you,' he tells *Didi*. 'But if your parents had been alive, they would have spanked you. And probably punished you severely as well. As it is, I really don't know what to do with you.'

'But I didn't spit in his food,' *Didi* says insistently, not seeming very repentant or concerned about *Dadu's* words.

'You spat in his food?' *Dadu* says, turning questioningly to *Munshiji*. 'Isn't there a limit to your bad behaviour?'

'Yes, *saab*, she got upset because I scolded her. You know how she gets into a rage.'

After a pause *Dadu* says, 'This really is too much, *dida*. You're growing up.

You can't just keep acting on impulse. I'm grounding you this evening. No fireworks today for you. And you'll stay home when we go to visit the temple later tonight.'

3.7

It is November 1963. Now that the weather is pleasant, *Dadu* has restarted my education about some of the architectural highlights of north India.

The previous year, we visited the beautiful temples and *ghats* of Bithoor, near Kanpur. This is the mythological site of the origin of the Hindu universe. We also saw the Valmiki *Ashram*, where Sita is supposed to have lived after her banishment by Rama, and where, so folklore has it, the *Ramayana* was composed.

This was followed by a trip to the breathtakingly beautiful marble work of Dilwara Temple in Mount Abu, as well as the fabled palaces and forts of Rajasthan, so alive in my imagination these many years already through the romance and chivalry of Rabindranath and Abanindranath Tagore's stories and poems and paintings for children, as well as those in *Sandesh* magazine.

Today, we are visiting the Bara or Asafi Imambara Complex in Lucknow.

As always, Guruji accompanies us. He and *Dadu* seem inseparable to my still-childish eyes. Many years later, long after *Dadu's* death, Guruji will refer to the bond he shared with him as 'the closest friendship of my life, almost a communion of souls'.

Accompanying us today are two guests. One is the famous Bengali writer and critic Syed Mujtaba Ali. And the other visitor, also from Calcutta, is Sureshwari Devi.

The Whispered Raga

We visit the mosque's vaulted central chamber and are startled by its size and the fact that it has no supporting beams. The guide tells us that it is the largest such structure in the world. And the ornate carving of the dome and hallway rival the stunning marblework I have seen at the Dilwara Temple. The guide points out the geometric perfection of the structure and the brilliance of its decorations in stone, marble inlay and stained glass.

The waters of the Gomti gleam through the sculpted arched windows as we walk into the first of the chambers of the *bhulbhulayah* or labyrinth. '*Dadu*, Guruji!' I say excitedly. 'It's as romantic as Chittorgarh and Udaipur.' The maze of chambers with the attached step-well or *bhowli*, and the three, mile-long passageways with their legends of romantic assignations and heroic battles long past do not disappoint us.

Our guests are still tired from their train journey, so we decide to return home early. On the way back, *Dadu* insists that Sureshwari Devi stay with us. We drive to her hotel and, over her loud protestations, pick up her things and continue homewards.

3.8

The following day, *Dadu* and Guruji arrange a meeting at Hazratganj with the nonagenarian *ustad* son of Nawab Wajid Ali Shah's court singer Chote Munne Khan whom we once visited in his hut. This, we all agree, will be an added treat for our Calcutta visitors.

All around us is a milling crowd of shoppers and university students decked out in their finest, strolling the stretch of the Mall between Mayfair and Benbow. Lucknow, still the garden city of Wajid Ali Shah's and British times, seems decked out in its finest this December morning.

As the Ustad alights from his hired carriage, *Dadu* rushes forward to pay the fare, while Guruji and I support his frail figure as he shuffles into the coffeehouse which is our pre-arranged rendezvous. It is packed, but we are led to a corner table marked 'Reserved'.

Dadu is in his court attire, with the black coat and bow-tie accentuating his sculpted features and philosopher's forehead. Even Guruji has donned a three-piece suit today, tailored by the venerable W. R. Draper, Clothiers and Haberdashers. He has a business meeting later to seek funds for Marris College, soon to be rechristened after its founder, Pandit Bhatkhande.

The adults talk about this and that for some time, of our visit to the open-air zoo in Banarasibaag, the delights and fragrances of Secundrabaag's sundry species of guavas, the bugles of the military police drill merging into the sweet winter sun peeping through the lingering late-morning fog, the recently remastered recordings of Zohrabai's *khayals*, and Chaplin's re-released City Lights.

The waiter, colourful in his china-silk waistcoat and cummerbund, brings out cucumber sandwiches with the menus. After we order, the talk drifts naturally to the music world of the Ustad's youth.

I have been listening patiently, but now I burst in, 'What was it like, Ustadji, in the old days? What was the music world really like then?'

The Ustad gives me a kindly smile and pats my head as he exchanges glances with Dadu and Guruji. 'I'll tell you, *beta*, but let me begin with some stories first. Things I know Mukherjee *saab* and Vishnuji want to hear about.'

He puckers his brows, closes his eyes and leans his surprisingly spry frame forwards in a gesture of concentration. After a few minutes, he says, 'Let me begin with something connected to one of the saddest chapters in our city's history.

'Faiyaz Khan was singing. It was around 1925 or so, although I can't exactly remember. It may have been at the Grand Conference organised by Bhatkhandeji at the Kaiserbagh Baradari. I was holding the *tanpura* behind him. He turned to me and said, "The audience is tired of listening to *dhrupad* and *dhamar* for the last two days." And he launched into a *thumri*. But what a *thumri*! *Babul mora naihar chuto jaye* – O my babul, my nest is vanishing.'

'Wajid Ali Shah's own composition as he leaves his beloved Lucknow en route to his banishment to Calcutta,' I say.

'Yes, *beta*, and at the Baradari which Wajid Ali Shah himself had built at Kaiserbagh into probably the most beautiful city in the world at that time. And which was ruthlessly sacked and then systematically demolished – just like the Red Fort in Delhi – by the British vandals to a mere shell of its former self.'

'And his listeners, the *nawabs* and *taluqdars* of Lucknow all knew this intimately as part of their family histories,' adds Guruji. 'And even European travellers who had seen Istanbul and Rome and Paris marvelled at Lucknow's beauty before it was sacked.'

'As Faiyaz sang, he would pause and recite the *shair* "*Daro deewaar par hasrat-se nazar karte hain, khush raho ehle watan, hum to safar karte hain*" – "I look longingly upon these walls; be happy, oh Time, for I am about to embark on my travels,"' continues the *ustad*, referring to the equally immortal, contemporaneous words of the exiled Sultan of Delhi Bahadur Shah Zafar before his own exile to Rangoon. He then pauses, seemingly overcome by emotion. We watch him silently. After a couple of minutes, he continues, 'And half of the people in the room were wiping the tears from their eyes. And then Faiyaz told the story of how the great *Ustad* Muzaffar Khan's family had travelled to Delhi. The Ustad was born before the Sepoy uprising of 1857. His father Ustad Maste Khan had taken refuge in Jaipur when Bahadur Shah Zafar was exiled to Rangoon. During the 1857 uprising, his grandfather Ustad Ali Baksh, the Delhi court singer, had stayed on in Calcutta. He was a guest at the court of the imprisoned Nawab Wajid Ali Shah in Metiabruz. So he sent for his son and grandson Maste Khan and Muzaffar Khan to be brought to Calcutta.'

Dadu asks, 'So how did they manage though. Delhi and all of the Kanpur and Lucknow region were in absolute turmoil, weren't they?'

The *ustad* smiles and then says, 'Yes, Faiyaz told the story of how they journeyed to Delhi, which was then being systematically looted and demolished by the British, arriving after two weeks on camels and bullock carts. From there, they boarded a *kisti* boat on the Yamuna. People were also dying of hunger across the United Provinces and especially around Lucknow. So they immediately embarked by boat along the Ganges for Gaya, foraging for fruits and vegetables along the riverbank.'

The *ustad* now pauses again, as though trying to remember. I break in, 'And after that, what happened after that?'

The *ustad* smiles indulgently at me and continues, 'Faiyaz said that from there the journey to Calcutta was less eventful, and food was once again available in the *mandis* and markets. They arrived at Calcutta's Metiabruz *ghat* via Patna, a full three-and-a-half months after leaving Delhi.'

'And after that, what happened after that?' I asked again, even more excitedly.

'On finishing his story, Faiyaz looked towards his audience. And then back at me. I had stopped my accompaniment. And he saw that I was crying profusely. *Hai*, what days those were! There will never be anything to rival them.'

After a hushed, pregnant, seemingly interminable pause, the *ustad* shakes his head. Then straightening himself in his seat, he continues, 'But let me tell you some stories about Bhatkhandeji himself. Mukherjee *saab* was asking me about him the other day.'

'Yes, yes,' says *Dadu*. 'I've heard that he was an incomparable storyteller.

'How can I describe him or his storytelling?' the Ustad seems to reminisce as he leans back and stares at the ceiling. 'You knew immediately that you were in the presence of someone extraordinary. Someone who didn't just know every nuance of north India's musical heritage but actually lived and breathed it. Bhatkhandeji would speak to us as contemporaries or equals, no matter who we were. But what stories he told, so rich in colour and life and resonance.'

'Tell us one, Ustadji,' says Guruji. 'I've heard from Pandit Ratanjankar that Bhatkhandeji often told stories of his youth. Or of the old *ustads* of the Gwalior court, and stories that he had heard from them about the court of Madhoji Scindia.'

'I will,' says the Ustadji. 'But what of your guests from Calcutta? They've been silent listeners all this while. What will they think of our famed Luckhnavi courtesy if all they have to do is to hear the ramblings of an old coot like me? How about giving them the floor?'

'Oh, Mujtaba here is a famous storyteller,' *Dadu* responds, gesturing towards our guest. 'Actually, he's an accomplished writer. Mujtaba, the floor's yours. Regale us.'

Mujtaba Ali smiles and begins in the inimitable, witty *majlishi* raconteur style which I would come to know intimately later. 'Let me tell you some stories about

Faiyaz Khan then,' he says. 'He's the one singer who actually showed me

Heaven on this Earth so many times. No one else has, either before or since.'

There are murmurs of agreement and nods of heads around the table and *Dadu* says, 'What an incomparable voice he had! You felt that there was a pair of *miraj tanpura*s resonating inside his stomach each time he closed his lips. I've never heard another such rich, resonant bass voice, with overtones that made the walls rattle.'

'Do you know that he once sang for Rabindranath Tagore at his ancestral home in Jorasankho, Calcutta?' Mujtaba Ali asks.

When the others shake their heads and shrug, he continues, 'That's only because we're from this benighted country. The European equivalent would be a meeting between Goethe and Beethoven. A historic meeting. Anyway, let me tell you of a *mehfil* in my Baroda home in honour of a lady family friend from Calcutta which Faiyaz graced with his presence. He was in great good spirits that day.'

'He usually was, wasn't he?' says Guruji. 'I've seen few great *ustads* who were as gracious and generous under all circumstances, and to the humblest of people.'

Mujtaba Ali nods and continues, 'It was 114 degrees that Baroda afternoon.

And still two months to the start of the monsoons. And someone requested that he sing his incomparable *raga Megh-Malhar*.'

'This sounds like the Tansen legends. Or Baiju Bawra,' says Sureshwari Devi with a smile, contributing to the conversation for the first time.

'Except that I saw it with my own eyes. He sang that day as though he was pouring out all his training, every ounce of creativity and all of his inborn and learnt skill into that hypnotic musical web. And we were sitting there silent and breathless, sucking in that sweetness through all the pores of our bodies.'

'When suddenly there were a few drops of rain outside, right?' Sureshwari Devi says. 'I've heard this story too.'

Mujtaba Ali acknowledges her with a nod and then continues, 'There was commotion all around. I don't have the power to describe who feted the *Ustad* in what manner, who cartwheeled on the floor like a pumpkin versus those who only stared at him with unblinking eyes. Only those with supernatural storytelling skills can do justice to supernatural events.'

'And what did Faiyaz Khan himself say, Mujtaba uncle?' I ask.

'He was strangely silent for a long time after everyone had left. And then he asked me in an almost melancholy tone, "Syed *sahib*, tell me why people embarrass me like this? Can I really bring down the rains with my singing?"'

'And what did you reply, uncle?'

'Well, without a moment's thought, I replied, "Only Allah knows about that. I only know that, at least tonight, he wanted to uphold your reputation."'

The elders continue exchanging reminiscences of the great *Ustad* for some more time, of how he had tamed a crowd of peasants near Kanpur by the magic of his voice, his devotion to Krishna which was so often expressed through his incomparable *Nom Tom* or *Hari Om Ananta Narayan alaap*.

Then Mujtaba Ali laughs and says, 'But this story of Faiyaz Khan will be incomplete if I don't mention his Ustad Jagadguru Mullick of Calcutta. This great man owned a foreign liquor store in Dharmatala. And he was also the guru of the legendary instrumentalists Hafiz Ali Khan and Enayat Khan.'

'What about him?' asks Guruji as we smile.

'I've seen this Jagadguru do *taans* and *sargam* covering five octaves while standing in that liquor store. There are existing 78 rpm discs, so this isn't a tall tale.'

'And these great *ustads* would go there?' I ask.

'Yes *beta*. They would park their horse and carriage outside his store, and then Faiyaz Khan would usually touch the so-called Jagadguru's feet and ask for instruction on some complex musical piece or ornament or the other.

In the meantime, Hafiz Ali would be busy selecting bottles and dumping them into his basket behind Faiyaz's broad back.'

The room erupts into laughter. Mujataba Ali waits patiently until the guffaws die and then adds, 'Actually, whenever they passed through Calcutta, all the famous *ustads* who were into a bit of the liquid stuff, the elixir of life you know, would make their pilgrimages to Dharmatala for this legendary Jagadguru's "blessings".'

There is another ripple of merriment all around. Then turning towards the old Ustad, Guruji says, "But we should return to you now, Ustadji. Tell us about Bhatkhandeji himself, of his musical accomplishment. Could you give us some idea of that, Ustadji?'

The Ustad shakes his head. He once again squints his eyes and furrows his brows as he dives into his ocean of memories. Then he says, 'Let me try to tell you – if I can put it into words – the most extraordinary musical encounter I have ever had. And my family traces its musical lineage back to the court of the Emperor Akbar on my mother's side,' he adds after a short pause.

Everyone nods and he continues, 'I remember that it was evening and I had gone to Bhatkhandeji's room. He was sitting silently as though deep in a trance. We knew that he had slowly been going deaf, but I realised that day that he no longer heard at all in either ear. And I suddenly, foolishly, burst out, "Panditji, isn't your deafness a great inconvenience to you?" I was much younger then, you know.'

'And what was his reply?' asks Guruji so softly that he is almost inaudible.

'He replied, "No, *beta*, it doesn't bother me at all. Last night I suddenly remembered an old *raga* I had heard fifty years ago. It appeared before me again yesterday in its full glory. And I immediately began singing it exactly as I had heard it then. It is a very rare *raga* – *raga Mangal*." Saying this, he again fell silent, although his ruminations seemed to continue with full force!'

3.9

Sureshwari Devi is visiting us at the Marris College today, during one of her periodic trips to the city of her birth.

I am now old enough to fully appreciate her presence. Grown men at the college blush while speaking of her appearance and charms. She is so fair that the red betel juice in her mouth shows through her skin when she chews *paan*. It is said that the *shairs* of the time proclaimed, 'A nubile young thing bereft of beauty and a city without Sureshwari are equally laid desolate.'

Rumour has it that she had gone for a spin in her coach-and-four one evening in Calcutta. She was stopped by the police since no one other than the governor was allowed a team of more than two horses. In the hoary lore of the school's old-timers, she is said to have tapped the cheek of the sergeant who stopped her in her imperious manner and said, 'Send your governor to me. He should forbid Sureshwari Devi in person.'

****

The famous *rabab* player from Afghanistan, Reza Ali Khan, is visiting the school. With his Greek God features and flowing locks, he cuts a very dashing figure.

When I first see him, he is accompanied by Sureshwari Devi. They seem inseparable and always wear perfectly colour-coordinated outfits whose psychedelic shades seem to leap out at us from the sea of nondescript attire at the school. Sureshwari Devi has never seemed more joyful. She is positively beaming at all of us.

The Whispered Raga

It takes my youthful mind some days to realise that they are in love. I think the day it finally sinks in is when I see Reza Khan sporting a small diamond in his left earlobe matching Sureshwari Devi's.

The next time I see them, they are rehearsing together in the green room, sitting hand-in-hand and looking into each other's eyes adoringly. Sureshwari is teaching Reza Khan a *ghazal*. His voice sounds reedy and hesitant compared to the resonant bass of the melodies that emanate from his *rabab*.

What follows over the next few weeks is astonishing even by Sureshwari Devi's rigorous standards. They rise at 4 a.m. each day and practice for four hours, and then bathe and sit down for breakfast. This is followed by *taalim* again from nine till one in the afternoon, and then lunch and a nap. On days when there is no formal or informal programme at the school, the evening features another extended session of *riyaaz*.

****

Sometime later, *Dadu* tells me that they have gone on a pilgrimage to Ajmer, and will continue from there to other sites in Himachal Pradesh and Kashmir.

Some weeks later, Sureshwari Devi is back at the school. She seems drawn and haggard. There is no sign of Reza Khan.

As I enter the school the next morning, Guruji dashes past me. To my surprise, he doesn't utter a word of greeting. I later learn that early that morning Sureshwari Devi attempted suicide by drowning herself in the Gomti River.

She is alive but has had a very close shave. By great good fortune, a *sadhu* performing his morning practices at the *ghats* on the riverbank plunged in and dragged her out in the nick of time.

****

About a month later, Reza Ali Khan resurfaces at the school. He looks like a man carrying the weight of the world on his shoulders. His colourful *sherwanis* and carefully parted hair have been replaced by the unkempt dress and tousled locks of a vagabond. Or a pining lover. Like the *deewana* of legend, he has been scrawling poetic graffiti extolling Sureshwari Devi in bold letters over the walls and pavements next to the school.

****

We are sitting for dinner at the school after a concert. Sureshwari has retired to her rooms to refresh her toilette which has taken on a new elaborateness since her attempted suicide.

She emerges an hour later, exquisite in white silk, diamonds flashing fire from her ears, throat and wrists. Her dark, *surma*-lined eyes and carefully rouged face are quite impassive. She has a small vial of *attar* – Lucknow's famed rose essence – clutched inside a handkerchief in her right palm.

About an hour later, Guruji turns towards Reza Ali Khan and asks, 'Reza *bhai*, how different is the *tip* or finger placement for the *rabab* from the *sarod*?'

Reza Ali Khan, his face puffed up with drink, is just about to reply when Sureshwari Devi jumps in, 'Gentlemen, let's forget all this. He's a slave to *ragas*. Certainly not their master.' She rises sharply to her feet, flinging the vial of *attar* to the ground as she storms out of the room.

****

The next morning, a body hangs limply from the large *neem* tree at the corner of the school yard, on the grassy knoll sloping away to the east. As the morning sun rises, there is a glint of light from the left ear.

3.10

A crowd of boys in grey shorts, white shirts and striped green ties are milling about the courtyard of St. Xavier's Collegiate School in Calcutta. *Dadu* is getting on in years and my grandmother is no more. He has decided that it will be better for my education if I move to Calcutta with Guruji who will now be both my guardian and my music teacher.

The school bell rings out insistently over the bustle. The boys begin lining up in front of their classrooms and the monitors shepherd them inside. Our teacher holds up his hand, motioning us to be silent just as I see Sureshwari Devi, dressed in her finest, appear at the classroom door. She has a boy in tow. It is her son Nazrul.

3.11

It is some months later. Nazrul and I are sitting next to each other during the post-lunch study period at school. Our attention, like that of everyone else in class, is concentrated on the current scene in the long-running battle that has raged all year between the supervising teacher, Mr. Cherian, and his bête noire Farley Gomes. There is little love lost between our class and Mr. Cherian who was our class teacher the previous year. In fact, most of the class are outraged by his blatant favouritism towards the two boys, Leslie and Ravi, who signed up for the Europe trip which he had organised the previous summer.

'Why are you officiating as monitor, Farley?' barks Mr. Cherian, stalking into the classroom.

'The boys asked me, sir,' replies Farley, all sweetness and sunshine.

'You return to your seat,' barks Cherian again, alive to the jibe that lies behind the honeyed tones. 'Leslie, you come and be the monitor,'

As there is a chorus of protests all around, Christopher Donaldson, now spending his sixth year in class eight while captaining both the middle school's hockey and football teams, gets to his feet. 'The fan always squeaks whenever Leslie's the monitor, sir. He can't seem to make it stop,' he tells Cherian, motioning his bosom friend Siddhartha with his left hand.

As Mr. Cherian turns red, the class is rent by a high-pitched squeaking. Everyone around Siddhartha, who is industriously rubbing a piece of Styrofoam on his watch-strap, is doubled up with laughter.

'See, sir,' says Farley innocently. 'It's already started.'

'It knows, sir,' someone else adds from the back of the classroom. 'It didn't like the snap Leslie brought back from Italy where you were all sprawled out on the deck of a steamer at the foot of the chair where Gina Lollobridgida was sunbathing.'

'You boys watch it,' Cherian snarls through clenched teeth. 'I'm reaching the end of my patience. As for you, Farley, one more wisecrack out of you and I'll take you to the Prefect of Discipline.'

****

It is some months later. Teachers' Day this year has featured skits about our biology teacher, Mr. Sen, followed by a thinly-disguised cameo about Farley and Cherian and ending in the former knocking out the latter with a Coca Cola spiked with an Aspirin 'mickey'.

Now Mr. Sen is supervising the study period. The boisterousness of the morning is continuing with everything except study being pursued in the room.

The mild-mannered Mr. Sen attempts to silence the din a few times in his halting English. Farley raises his hand and with an expression of the greatest seriousness says, 'Sir, sir, I have some questions about the last bio lesson.'

Mr. Sen replies with equal earnestness, 'Yes, Pahrley,' pronouncing his name in the typical Bengali fashion. 'But you must come to me when I am empty.'

This sally is met with hoots of laughter and the launch of two paper planes from opposite sides of the room set on a collision course above his head.

Throwing up his hands in perplexed vexation, he cries, 'You boys! Jumping horse, eating grass, no!'

His literal translations from Bengali are legendary throughout the school, and this rendering of the proverb meaning something akin to 'Putting the cart before the horse' arouses fresh merriment.

Perhaps thinking that use of the national language might carry more weight, Mr. Sen switches hurriedly to a torrent of broken Hindi in his decidedly Bengali accent. Then, frustrated by the lack of response, he finally brings the house down by blurting out the weightiest word in his English lexicon in a surprisingly coherent sentence, 'Introspect, introspect! You must introspect, gentlemen!'

Seeing the bellows and hoots of laughter that his latest sally has triggered, he charges out yelling, 'You don't listen! I'm going to fetch Mr. Cherian.'

3.12

Guruji and I are in one of the Sursagar School of Music's rehearsal rooms.

Some of Calcutta's greatest musicians are assembled here for a special recording session arranged by All India Radio. They include the famed sitar player Badal Khan, vocalist Idanbai, as well as the violinist Bamacharan Banerjee, a student of the khayal style of Wajid Ali Shah's last *ustads* Taj Khan and Ali Baksh Khan at his court-in-exile in Metiabruz in Calcutta.

The door opens and Sureshwari Devi steps regally into the room. As usual, she is dressed to the hilt. She surveys the room as Guruji ushers her to a seat in the corner.

An outdoor marquee has been built on the front lawn of the school.

Ustad Badal Khan first takes his place on the colourful raised platform. A jungle of microphones and wires is strung all around him.

He begins with the ethereal *raga Puriya*, which his father Ustad Mansoor Khan had perfected before him. Midway through the performance, an official of All India Radio runs up onto the stage and gently motions the *Ustad* and his accompanists to move away from the microphones. Volume controls are still rudimentary and the *gat* and *jhala* will sound too loud otherwise.

At around seven in the evening, the Ustad starts the *alaap* for *raga Behag*. An hour later when he finishes, I have a feeling that a dark genie is in our midst, screaming out some primal agony through the strains pouring from the wailing strings. Every hair on my body is standing straight up and I am impaled to the seat. As the *ustads* of old were wont to say, 'The *raga* has come alive and is standing before us.'

Nazrul leans over to me as the *Ustad* brings the *raga* to a close. 'My mother told me that he was playing this *raga* on the day one of his daughters died,' he says. As he whispers the words and the music stops, my numbness melts away and I feel as though I can move once again. I then look around the marquee. There are tears in every eye.

The *Ustad* seems lost to the world for a few minutes. Tears are streaming profusely down his cheeks, and into his henna-dyed beard and moustache. He rises to his feet, bows low to the audience and murmurs quickly, '*Mujhe is Behag ke liye bahut bhari qurbani dena para.*' ('I had to make a very heavy sacrifice for this Behag.') Then he gently steps off the stage.

****

A feast fit for a king has been laid out on the lawn. AIR has certainly spared no expense for this occasion.

I am standing with Nazrul, Guruji and Sureshwari Devi. Idanbai approaches us and smiles. I am surprised when she asks Sureshwari Devi, 'What will you be recording, Sureshwari? I'm look forward to hearing you next.'

Sureshwari Devi seems taken aback. She gathers herself to her full height, saying, 'It's a piece for *khandaani* musicians, not just any casual listener.'

Idanbai responds quietly, 'You can take this tone even after hearing Ustadji's *Behag*. We've been at each other's throats a long time. We teach at the same school. And we're not young any more. Why not just make peace?'

'I don't cast pearls before swine. It takes generations of breeding to understand my music.' Sureshwari Devi is even more blunt this time. She wheels around and strides off.

I am left marvelling yet again at her generations of breeding.

3.13

A group of boys are clustered together in the class nine classroom waiting for their first social with their sister school, the nearby Loreto House Convent. Farley has a large photograph clutched to his chest, face-down. 'Hey guys. Guess what this is,' he says to the boys crowded near him.

There are shouts and a melee, and the photograph is torn from his hand and falls to the floor. It is an enlargement of 'the picture' and it has whetted our curiosity all year. It features Mr. Cherian and his brood of protégés, including our classmates Leslie and Ravi, squatting on the deck of a steamer somewhere in the Mediterranean. And the deckchair right behind them is occupied by a bikini-clad Gina Lollobridgida no less. How even as canny a customer as Mr. Cherian scooped that particular shot has engaged our collective imaginations ever since we first laid eyes on it a few weeks before in class.

There are some wolf whistles and cries. And then, just as Farley dives to the floor to scoop it up, the first girl walks through the door. Behind her are five others. They smile at Farley comically bent over making a grab for the picture. Then their smiles freeze as their eyes alight on the scene it portrays. Farley's outstretched fingers and the muscles framing the silly smile pasted to his lips appear to have been overcome by a sudden onset of rigor mortis.

And now another girl walks through the door. She is holding a bouquet of flowers. As she hurries over to the vase placed in the centre of the table, a Beatles song crackles through the rented PA system. The party has officially begun.

Nazrul whispers to me, 'That's Lopa, Idanbai's daughter. My mother is dead set against the idea, but she and her mother will be joining the music school next month. At least that's what Guruji said.'

'I heard that too,' I whisper back. 'But I've never seen her before.'

'She's nice-looking like her mother. And she seemed pleasant when I met her at music conferences in the past. Even though our mothers usually flash daggers at each other with their eyes. At least, my mother does.'

'Look, she's dropped a rose.' We hurry forward to pick it up.

'Here Lopa, you dropped this,' says Nazrul, stepping forward and handing it to her.

'Thanks a lot, Nazrul,' she says. 'I didn't notice you before, although I knew that you'd be here. I was hurrying because I felt so stupid having to put the bouquet into a vase with rock music blaring out all around. It feels so incongruous. But Sister Damacin insisted that I should.'

'This is my best friend Aniket,' Nazrul says, pointing to me.

'Hi Aniket,' says Lopa, smiling.

I am suddenly tongue-tied, as if all the blood has drained away from my face and chest. My reply sticks in my throat. Even given my adolescent shyness, this is somehow different.

3.14

Nazrul and I are walking down Park Street with some school friends. In the distance, near the crossing of Middleton Row, we spy a group of girls wearing the distinctive grey and white Loreto House uniform. I spot Lopa in the group and, with an abrupt nudge to Nazrul and saying nothing at all to my other friends, dash off to see her.

As they head down Middleton Row, I catch up with them in front of the Kalimpong Home Products bakery. 'Hi Lopa,' I say, a tad out of breath.

Lopa is surprised but she introduces me to her friends. I am too confused to even properly acknowledge their greetings. I stare at them in bewilderment, searching for something to say. 'I saw you from a distance,' I finally blurt out. 'I guess you're heading back to school.'

'Yes,' Lopa says. 'We came out after lunch for some *churan* and *amsat*.'

I am again at a loss for words and am relieved when Nazrul strides up. We converse for a few more minutes and then part. As we head back towards Park Street, Nazrul asks, 'You seem agitated, Aniket?' I look at him wordlessly and he is silent as well. But I can see comprehension dawning in his eyes.

'I'm such an idiot, Nazrul. I freeze whenever I'm in the presence of girls.'

'And especially Lopa. That's how it is, is it?'

I nod. As we rejoin the group, our friends rib me about my sudden 'tryst'.

'Tell us, Aniket,' says Farley mischievously, affecting a pompous tone. 'Who was that?'

'Oh, it's a friend from our music school,' I say casually.

But twenty minutes later, when we are settled in Kwality's Café, sipping cold coffees – after testing the front door of Mag's and finding it closed – the jokes are far from over.

'You're a deep customer,' says Farley. 'Still waters run deep, huh!'

'Or "Sinking, sinking, drinking water" as Mr. Sen would say,' adds Siddhartha to gales of laughter, referring to the Bengali aphorism to the same effect.

'Tell us her name,' says Farley as there is chorus of cries of 'Ya, ya!' for the next few minutes.

Finally Siddhartha chimes in, 'He's stonewalling, guys. Let's name her Kavita.'

There is a renewed chorus of cries and then someone adds, 'Aniket loves Kavita. Someone in our class sure does love poetry!'

3.15

I am inside one of the old London-style telephone booths that still remain in central Calcutta, outside the Hall and Anderson department store at the Park Street-Chowringhee crossing. Nazrul is waiting outside, staring out towards the Asiatic Society, periodically swivelling around a bit to look in the direction of the Trincas café, the Oxford Bookstore and then towards the Mansukhani Jewellers and the Castlewood sports stores under the Queens Mansions awnings a little past the crossing of Park and Russell Streets.

'Hullo, hullo,' I speak into the phone. 'Can I speak to Lopa, please?'

'Who is that speaking?' I recognise Idanbai's voice.

'It's me, auntie. It's Aniket,' I reply.

'What do you want with Lopa, *beta*?' she asks.

'Oh, we met at the school social last month, auntie. And I just wanted to talk to her.'

'Oh.' There is a pause. 'All right, hold the line, *beta*. I'll see if she's in.'

In a few minutes, Lopa comes to the phone. 'Hi Aniket,' she says.

I'm not sure what comes over me suddenly. Perhaps it is the accumulated thoughts and feelings of the past weeks. I blurt out, 'I act like an idiot when I see you, Lopa. I know I do, like that day on Middleton Row. But I just can't get you out of my head. I keep thinking of you all the time, including first thing in the morning and last thing at night.'

There is a long pause. I wait breathlessly for her reaction. She says quietly, 'Mother won't like this, you know,' not revealing her own feelings at all.

I feel crushed. My mind is in a whirl. I summon all my courage and concentration and say, 'But auntie likes me, Lopa. She is always so kind to me at the school, and is full of encouragement and praise all the time.'

After another pause, Lopa says, 'Yes I know. She talks of your singing. Praises you very highly. But she won't like this.'

'But why, Lopa? Why? Is it because I'm Hindu, Lopa? Or at least I am by birth. Is that it?'

'It's not that simple, Aniket. It would take too long to explain it now. Ammi will wonder if we talk that long. I'll tell you some other time.'

'But you must tell me, Lopa. At least, give me some idea of why she would object. You know that I don't care two hoots about religion.'

Lopa is silent for a minute. Then she says, 'She's suffered in life, Aniket. Because she was born in a *mirasi* family, the lowest of the low in the music world.'

'But why should that concern us now, Lopa? We live in a different world.

I'm not from that world anyway. And my family wouldn't care about any differences in our backgrounds. As it is, *Dadu* was always a social rebel of sorts. Idanbai knows him. She knows that, doesn't she? And *Didi*'s in Australia and she couldn't care less either about such things.'

'It's an irrational thing, Aniket. She's been hurt all her life. And she's afraid that I may be as well. I really must be going now. Is there anything else?'

'No,' I reply lamely. There is a polite, impersonal 'bye' from both ends and we hang up.

3.16

I am on a walk around the lakes with Nazrul and Prem Kishan. It is two days before Durga Puja and, as in the rest of the city, the area is bustling with preparations. Tempos carrying statues of the goddess and her consorts, made of every material imaginable, to the *pandals* or marquees sprouting on all sides.

Each year, these neighbourhood *pujas* vie to outdo each other in innovativeness and illumination. This time, there is already a buzz surrounding some, including an image built entirely of matchsticks in a *pandal* shaped like the mouth of an erupting volcano, and another of razor blades housed in a structure modelled on the giant Buddhist *stupa* at Sanchi.

We skirt the larger lake and cross over the railway tracks into Jodhpur Park. Crowds of holiday shoppers and revellers spill out from the gates of the newly-built Dakshinapan Handicraft Complex, displacing the vendors who normally dominate the area. Enveloped by the songs blaring from the loudspeakers, even the battered trams and buses seem to sport a festive look as they trundle past, robed in the multi-coloured hues of the *pandal* lights.

We have a radio programme later in the afternoon at the Doordarshan building near Dalhousie Square and the Strand. But we need a bite to eat before that. The *shami kababs* from the Chat Ghar run by some Punjabi ladies in their garage on a small side-street are one of our favourites, but it is closed. So we settle on the little Chinese restaurant next to it.

****

We are at the radio station. It has been weeks since I have seen Lopa. Now, Idanbai is inside the recording studio with Guruji. The four of us talk for some time. Then, Lopa rises. To my surprise, she motions to me with her hands behind Nazrul and Prem's backs indicating that I follow her. I see her disappear down the corridor. After a few minutes, I get up and walk in the same direction.

As I duck into the door where her palms peep out, beckoning me into the room, she rushes forward, wraps me in an embrace and then gives me a quick peck on the cheek. I am startled. 'I so wanted to see you before we left for the holidays, Aniket,' she gushes.

'I know that you're leaving for Lucknow tomorrow,' I say, sounding a bit lame to my own ears. 'Guruji told me. But when can we meet again?'

'We'll be gone for the whole Puja holidays, Aniket. So not till school starts. And *Ammi's* trying to have me go to the Bhatkhande Music College after I finish school. We'll be visiting them while we're in Lucknow. And I'll probably have an audition there as well.'

'So that she can separate us,' I say. She nods. 'What'll I do without you, Lopa? Nazrul is leaving next week as well. It'll be a long three weeks.'

'I'll write, Aniket. I promise.'

'At least once a week. D'you promise?'

'Oh, much more than that. I promise. But we should go. The others will wonder what happened to us. And *Ammi* might come out too.' She leans forward and pecks me on the cheek again.

Once again, I am startled. She has never been this demonstrative before. I reach for her. But she moves away quickly, giggling. Then she sticks out her tongue at me and runs from the room.

3.17

Now that the vocal *jugalbandhis* of old times have returned following the more recent instrumental duets that are all the rage after Ravi Shankar and Ali Akbar Khan's joint recitals, Nazrul and I are practicing a new piece in one of the school's upstairs rehearsal rooms. Next door, we can faintly hear Sureshwari Devi rehearsing with a student.

There is a knock on the front door. It is the postman. We hear the door open.

A few minutes later, Guruji shouts from the bottom of the stairs, 'Aniket, *beta,* come, come down quickly!'

It is a letter from the Indian Institute of Technology. I am placed twenty first in the All India Entrance Examinations. The interview to choose the discipline of study is to be held at the Kharagpur campus in four weeks' time.

3.18

I spy Lopa waiting for me outside the cafeteria of the Arts Faculty of Jadavpur University. She is now a student in the Department of Comparative Literature there, but only until she hears back from Lucknow's Bhatkhande Music School. She is pacing back and forth with her head slightly bowed. She seems thoughtful, perhaps even nervous. Several other students look curiously in her direction.

She sees me as I cross the bridge and road and comes running up to me. 'How was it?' she asks, 'What did you decide on?'

'I chose electronics engineering for now. It's the most sought-after stream, you know.'

'But you're so keen on physics and mathematics! Besides you singing, it's all you do every minute of your waking day, Aniket.'

'Ah, but that's because a certain someone won't make time for me. Doesn't want to. But places the blame on her mother.'

Lopa laughs. 'But seriously, Aniket. Are you sure that's the right thing to do?'

I nod. 'They told me that it'd be easy to change to physics or mathematics after a year or two if I wanted to. But the reverse would be very difficult. Let's go and get a cup of tea. I rushed straight here from the station. The tea cups at Kharagpur(KGP) station are so tiny they wouldn't slake even a bird's thirst.'

'I can't today, Aniket. I've promised *Ammi* that I'll be home early.'

'Can I see her sometime soon? Will you ask her? Maybe this will make her change her mind.'

'It won't help,' Lopa says. She hesitates and then adds, '*Ammi's* trying to set me up with someone else. A senior student at the Bhatkhande School.'

'Is he Muslim?'

When she nods in reply I burst out, 'God, in this day and age! Whatever can be so wrong with being from different religions? And even though we couldn't care less. What's wrong with her! Why does she have it in for me?'

Lopa is silent. Then she puts a finger on my lips and says, 'Shh, Aniket. Calm down. Calm down. Let's not spoil our mood over someone else, even if she's my *ammi*. Her trying something doesn't mean that I'll agree.'

'OK, OK,' I say brusquely. My heart is still pounding. 'When can I see you again?'

'I'll try and call you at the school on Friday. I should know about my admission to Bhatkhande by then. Bye.' She squeezes my forearm quickly, waves and runs over towards the bus stop on the main road.

3.19

It is the following Friday evening. I have been waiting for Lopa's call all day. I pace up and down the long corridor wrapping around the eastern side of the Sursagar school courtyard. I see Lopa in my mind's eye. She is running to the bus stop. She waves and says, 'I'll call you.' And then the words that have been haunting me every minute since that day emerge from her lips, '*Ammi's* trying to set me up with someone else. A senior student at the Bhatkhande School.' I clench my fists and try to control the shudder that passes down my frame.

There is a knock on the front door. Perhaps it's her. Maybe, she has decided to come instead of calling. I streak across the grass to open it. But it is Guruji.

'What's up, son?' Guruji asks. My disappointment is written all too clearly on my face and body.

'Nothing, Guruji. It's nothing. Really...'

As I trail off in a less than convincing fashion, he asks softly, 'It's her. Lopa, right? You were expecting her.'

'Yes, Guruji.'

'You can tell me, son. It's easier when you let it out. Has anything else happened?'

'She said she would call, Guruji. I've been waiting all day.'

'And that's all? Maybe something came up. Or maybe their phone is dead. You know these Calcutta telephones during the monsoons.' But I continue to look uncertain, so he adds, 'Are you sure that's all, *beta*?'

I look into his eyes for a few moments before crying out, 'Oh no! No Guruji! What more could happen! Idanbai's trying to arrange a match for Lopa!' Tears sting my eyes as I bury my face in his shoulder.

3.20

Guruji has brought me for a walk to the lakes. 'There's nothing like nature to soothe the soul, *beta*,' he says as we turn off Southern Avenue, past the *bhel* and *panipuri* and juice vendors, towards the water's edge.

I am silent. Nayan, our favourite vendor of nuts and corn on the cob is doing his rounds, crying out, '*Bhutta, bhutta. Cha, cha, chai garam. Baadaam, baadaam,*' in the hoarse theatrical vocal bursts he affects when trying to attracts customers. He bustles forward to us, beaming from ear to ear in his usual effusive fashion. '*Cha neben, dada-babu? Chai, Guruji? Bhutta ekdom gorom. Ekkhuni shekechi kath-koilar opor.*' ('Do you want tea, *dada-babu* and Guruji? The corn's piping hot. I just roasted it on the coals.')

We buy some tea from him but decline the *bhutta* pleading lack of hunger. He stands around for a few minutes chatting about this and that. And then, presses the corn on us again. He seems unusually insistent today.

'Is anything the matter, Nayan?' I ask him. 'Why d'you keep offering us the *bhutta?*'

He seems taken aback by the question and then replies hesitantly, 'It's my daughter, *dada-babu*. She's been very ill.'

And then it all comes tumbling out. The familiar everyday story of the poor. He has been to the outdoor of the R. G. Kar Medical College, but the House Staff there have recommended that he take her to a nursing home. They want to help. But their hands are tied. The hospital is terribly overcrowded. There are no free beds to admit her and almost no medicines. The maintenance staff sells them on the black market. They are unionised and even the Superintendent cannot control them.

Guruji takes out a hundred rupee note and presses it on him. 'Come back and ask me for more if you need. I'll find it somehow. But go now. Right now. Take her to the doctor,' he says.

Nayan almost falls at Guruji's feet. Guruji taps him affectionately on the shoulder and says, 'Go, Nayan. Go quickly. Don't delay.'

Nayan presses the rest of the *bhuttas* on us and then makes off at a quick clip towards the railway lines bordering the lakes' far edge with the empty wicker basket and large kettle and cups swinging by his sides.

As we watch him leave, Guruji sighs, 'People have so many problems in this poor land of ours. And so much sadness.'

We stare out onto the lake. Two rowing teams are out on the water. And in the distance, we can hear the shouts of the swimmers inside Anderson Club. A few minutes later, one of the canoes scatters the ducks and swans teeming around the bridge adjoining the Lake Club.

'Do you know what your *Dadu* used to say when we were in Lucknow?' Guruji asks suddenly, catching me by surprise. I have been thinking of Lopa again.

'About what, Guruji?'

'He used to say, 'If the poor are indeed Narayan, or God, as we say in India, would one really want to go to Heaven?'

I realise that he is still thinking of Nayan. 'That does sound like *Dadu*,' I say. And then, unaccountably, I blurt out what has been on my mind all these days. Perhaps it is the mention of the old days. Or of *Dadu*. I tell Guruji everything. About Lopa. And Idanbai.

He listens to me carefully in his usual sympathetic fashion. After I finish, he puts his arms around my shoulders and squeezes them hard. 'I can't say that I'm completely surprised, *beta*,' he says. 'After all, I don't have all these grey hairs for nothing. I know that you've been preoccupied and restless. And I guessed that it might have something to do with Lopa. Even before you told me today about Idan trying to arrange a match for her.'

'But there must be some way to make her understand, Guruji, to make THEM understand,' I say.

'Listen, son. When I told your *Dadu* that I would take care of you, I knew that someday this issue too would arise. Except that I didn't anticipate that the girl would be so well-known to me.'

'But what should I do, Guruji? I can't even understand my feelings. They've taken over my life. I almost can't concentrate on anything else – my studies, my singing... Anything at all.'

'Love. It's one of the great mysteries of life, isn't it, *beta*? The greatest, except THE mystery of mysteries. But try not to think about it too much. At your age, all this is inevitable. But only time reveals the answers.'

'But why is Idanbai so adamant about this, Guruji? I know she has always been very fond of me.'

'She's had a very hard life, *beta*, very different from yours. It would be hard for you to really understand. Not the entire world of north Indian music is like our little circles in Lucknow or Calcutta. And Idan knows only the rigid ways of the society she was born into. She really doesn't believe that the outside world is different.'

'But can't you change her mind? Talk to her. Make her understand.'

Guruji smiles, 'Oh, Aniket. The impatience of youth! Just think of Nayan. Compare your troubles to what he deals with every day.'

I am silent for a while, then blurt out, 'But are they any less? How can you even say that they're not comparable to his?'

Guruji smiles and strokes my head. He says, 'I didn't say they weren't, Aniket. Life can be so unpredictable. And difficult. Stranger than fiction they say in English, right? Let me tell you a story, *beta*.'

I look away towards the water. 'Listen, *beta*,' says Guruji. 'And try to understand:

Once, a wanderer, on his travels, saw a gigantic old oak tree standing at the ocean's edge. He thought to himself, "This is a useless tree. If you make a ship from it, it will soon rot; if you make tools, they would break. You can't do anything useful with this tree and that's why it's grown so old."

Back at the inn that evening, when he was asleep, the oak tree appeared to him in a dream and said, "Why d'you compare me to cultivated trees, the ones which bear fruit? Even before they can ripen their fruit, people attack and violate them. Their branches are broken and their twigs ripped off. Their own gifts bring ruin and harm to them, and they cannot live out their natural span. This is what happens everywhere, and so I have long since stopped attempting to be of any use at all. That's why I've managed to survive and grow to this size."

The man asked the tree, "But what is the meaning of what you say?"

"Fulfilling your own destiny is the greatest achievement of all," the tree replied. "Not anything utilitarian. Forget that only at your peril."

"But how will I know my own destiny? How can one find that out?"

The tree replied, "Ask the ocean tomorrow and she will tell you."

The next day, the wanderer sat by the ocean's edge. He spent the entire day asking what his destiny was but received no answer.

That night, once again, he had a dream. The ocean appeared to him and said, "Ask me again tomorrow and you will find the answer."

The next day, a great storm rose. And the wind blew and the waves crashed onto the shore for many days. But the wanderer was determined to receive his answer. And so he stayed at his post, through the wind and the water and the thunder and lightning.

He stayed there day after day. His body grew gaunt, his clothes grew tattered, and still the storm showed no sign of abating. He was close to exhaustion and his food had run out and so had his money.

And then, one day, just as he was about to abandon his quest, the waves calmed and the wind quieted and the thunder ceased. And beneath the waves, ringing ever louder, he heard it: the whispered *raga*. It grew louder and louder, it made the trees quiver and the ground shake. And then it was so close that he fell down unconscious on the ground.

When he came to, everything was silent again. But he had his answer. He knew what he should do.'

In spite of my reluctance, I have been mesmerised by the story. I continue to look at Guruji for some time after he falls silent, trying to read his face and understand why he narrated it to me. I say, 'It had a hypnotic ring, Guruji. But what does it mean? How does one know one's destiny?'

'That is another of the great mysteries, *beta*. Like the mystery of mysteries. One of those questions before which all words recoil into silence. Like the mysterious smile on the Great Sphinx at Giza.'

'But surely the story is saying something, Guruji?'

'Yes, *beta*. Of course it is. It's saying that one must go to the ocean of life and listen. Through all the storms, one must wait and listen. And when the time and place are right, one will hear it, the whispered *raga* that points you to your very own lodestone, your personal Pole Star.'

'And do you listen for it, Guruji?' I ask.

'Music is my touchstone, *beta*. It is one of the great instruments to surrender and to listen.'

'But what has this story to do with what with we were talking about, with Lopa and me and Idanbai?' I am so impatient that the words come out with more force than I intend them to.

Guruji stares at me with a curious smile. He leans over and mutters softly, 'Love is another instrument, *beta*. A compass pointing you to your true north.'

3.21

The following day, I try calling Lopa all morning without success. Visits to her home and Jadavpur University prove abortive as well.

Now in the afternoon, I am back at the school. Guruji has just returned and I am waiting for him in the lobby. As he comes downstairs, I ask, 'Have you heard anything from Lopa, Guruji? Did she come? Or call?' I yip like an overenthusiastic puppy.

He nods, 'Yes, *beta*. Idanbai called.'

'And?'

'Lopa's been admitted to the Bhatkhande College. Idanbai thinks that it's best for you to be apart for some time.'

'But I can't even see her? What kind of inhuman behaviour is that?'

'*Beta*, in the circumstances, my advice is to be patient. You'll be going to IIT in a few months, anyway. Go there. Think about things. Keep in touch with Lopa. As I told you, time will reveal the answers to you.'

'I'm going to call Lopa. Right now.'

'Try, *beta*. See what happens. That's all I can say. Things might be easier with Idanbai in a few months. After you've been apart for some time, so that she's less fearful on a daily basis.'

'Fearful? But what's she afraid of, Guruji?'

'You know just as well as me, *beta*. Mostly of Lopa getting hurt.'

'But she'll ruin my life, Guruji! Our lives!'

'If it's meant to be, it will work out one way or the other. One day she will understand.'

'Oh, I know, I know. All that bunkum about "*Jonmo, mrityu, biye, tin shotyo niye*"' ("Birth, marriage, and death, we're born with three truths.")

Guruji smiles. But I can see that he is worried about me. He pulls me towards him and begins stroking my hair, repeating over and over again, '*Beta, beta, beta...*'

I lift my face as tears sting my eyes. 'Just you see, Guruji. I'll show her. I'll transfer to IIT Kanpur. So we'll be close together, Lopa and I. I'll show Idanbai!'

3.22

A cowed group of freshmen at IIT Kanpur, or 'freshers' as they are called, mill about in a room in one of the many hostels within the campus. After days of the IIT anthem, the imaginary chair, the scurrilous IIT versions of Newton's Laws and other assorted delights, we have a respite today.

A senior named Vaswani has picked up my hostel wingmates and me this evening from outside the Hall 2 mess right after tea and taken us to his room in Hall 5. He has a bed sheet wrapped around his head. 'I'm an Arab sheikh. Bow to me, freshers! Kowtow right now. Or I'll put you in my harem!' His eyes are twinkling.

Clearly, he has a sense of humour. As the evening progresses, we realise that this will be a very different sort of ragging, more shared entertainment than intimidation and humiliation.

After we are settled on the bed in his outsized room, in itself a change from days of squatting on the floor or standing bolt upright for evenings on end, he sends three of us into the three cubicles in the corner of his room. 'You're in IIT Kanyakumari,' he tells the unfortunate one who is squeezed into the space at floor level usually meant for shoes and dirty clothes. 'You'll give us an interesting quote from Swami Vivekananda's visit there, but better make it interesting. Okay, *yaar*?'

In the central area, in reality a closet with a door, is a fresher whose father is the owner of a leather factory in Kanpur city. 'You're the cuckoo clock, man,' Vaswani tells him in his languid drawl. 'Every thirty seconds, you'll open the door and alternately say "Kukru ku, I love you" and "My father is a dirty capitalist pig." OK? Got it, right?' The fresher has a hard time keeping a straight face and we are almost in splits.

'Now, you there, you man,' Vaswani says as he points his index finger with a flourish. 'Hey, ahoy there mate! Wake up, you. It can't be that cold up there in Simla!' The fresher on the top berth, so to speak, is giggling. 'Okay now, cool it a bit,' Vaswani says. 'You're the narrow gauge train taking the Viceroy up to his summer capital, right. So every time your pal down south quotes Vivekananda, the man below in the plains of Central India will emerge and howl out his thing. Whenever he says, "Kukru ku", you'll echo "Chooooooo, chooooooo, me too, me too!" And when he says, "My father's a dirty...." what'll you say? Come on man, give us a brainwave. We're really low on entertainment here."

The fresher is quick on the uptake. 'I'll say "Choooooo, chooooooo, I hear you, I hear you" sir,' he replies.

'That's great,' says Vaswani, gleefully rubbing his hands. 'You'll survive here. You have what it takes. But cut out the 'sir' crap, at least with me! OK guys, got it. One, two, three!'

The next ten minutes feature one continuous concert of Vivekananda, punctuated by the cuckoo clock and its faithful echo. Everyone else in the room is lying on the floor in stitches.

After it ends, Vaswani turns his attention floorwards. 'OK guys, your turn now. You there, what's your department?'

'Aero, sir,' the fresher coughs. 'I mean no sir, just Aero…..'

'Relax, *yaar*,' says Vaswani. 'I'm not going to bite you. Now look, your neighbour there is pregnant and just about to give birth. And your other friend is delivering the baby. But as an Aero man, at least an aspirant, it's your job to test the ventilation in the room. So you'll be doing your thing in the wind tunnel, testing the ventilation under the fan. But make it interesting, *yaar*, some real data and the jargon of the trade. Got it, guys?'

Looking at my neighbour, whose father has turned out to work in the Met office, he says, 'Now you, my friend. I have just the thing for you. Once the baby's out and the ventilation's been tested, you'll give us a five-minute speech on why your father is always wrong. But some real meat, man. Not just glib platitudes or curses. Got it?'

Finally it is my turn. 'You're the topper type, man, right?' he says as he eyes me from head to toe. 'Hmm, let's see. Let's see your real IQ, how you think on your feet. OK, you'll give us periodic updates, in between the delivery and the wind-tunnel experiments, on the effect of Golda Meir's periods on grasshoppers in the EU. OK, let's get set.

Take up your positions.'

The next hour is again an uninterrupted, raucous cacophony. By the time it is over, we are holding our sides in splits of laughter and tears are streaming from everyone's eyes.

****

It is about a year later. Lopa and I visit each other every month after she has moved to the Bhatkhande College in Lucknow, a stone's throw from Kanpur. We have never been happier. Or more free.

Today, she is visiting me at the IIT campus. I have come to the Girls' Hostel, or GH, to pick her up from the room of a friend where she has spent the night. As we walk out, she says, 'D'you know what happened this morning, Aniket?'

'How can I?' I say. 'But it's the ragging period. So I guess just about anything's possible.'

'Well, about six in the morning, a bunch of guys – freshers, I suppose, as you always call them – started singing outside the hostel.'

'Poor guys. It's really illegal. They're not supposed to be ragged during sleeping times. But who's checking? So what were they singing?'

'They were really yelling at the top of their lungs, "*Jago sone-walo*"' – Rise all you who sleep – 'But they didn't stop with that.'

'So what else did they do?'

'After a while, they switched to shouting "Hall 2-GH *bhai-bahen*. Hall 2-GH *bhai-bahen*"' Hall 2 and GH are brothers and sisters. 'And then...' She stops, blushing. 'I can't even bring it to my lips.'

'It's OK, Lopa, I know already. Hall 2 *behen-*...! Right? It's an IIT classic,' I say. 'Be thankful the senior wasn't dumb enough to make a fresher streak near the GH. It's the new fad this year.'

****

Another of Lopa's visits. She has accompanied my wingmates and me on a trip to Bithoor by tempo. What with singing at the tops of our voices all the way back and forth, and the picnic and carousing in Bithoor itself, it has been a wonderful day. We are pleasantly tired this evening as we enter our hostel.

But surprises await us. As we come up the stairs to our wing, we see that it is in total darkness. 'Someone's taken out the fuses, *yaar*,' one of my wingmates says. 'We'd better be on guard. I think a wing *punga's* brewing.'

Two minutes later, our jaws drop. Half our rooms' doors have vanished. And one room in the middle has swing doors instead, improvised from a couple of ventilator panels scavenged from their usual positions above the doors. No doubt the saloon doors in the western *Gunfight at the OK Corral* which was screened the previous Friday has provided the inspiration.

We enter through the swing doors to see just how much of the furniture has been disturbed, or in IIT parlance, how much the CG or centre of gravity has been changed. The next instant, there are whoops from the two darkened rooms on both sides. A mass of bodies comes rushing out at us and then we are all ankle-deep in water; they have dumped it on us by the bucketful.

Half an hour later, a full-scale war of the hostel wings is in progress. Our retaliation has been swift, but not before half the beds in our wing have also been doused with water. Now, a couple of hotheads have decided that we should retaliate in kind and that it is total war! The members of the rival wing have been put to flight after some hand-to-hand combat and are cowering at the far end of their own wing, awaiting our next line of action.

Half an hour later still. Several beds in our rivals' wing have been carted over the railings and are now lying on the hostel lawn three floors below. And we are all lined up before the hostel warden, a strict man now in a particularly foul mood after being woken up from his beauty sleep close to midnight by urgent summons.

The warden issues severe reprimands and exemplary punishment to a few of the ringleaders, those responsible for the call for all-out war.

****

Lunchtime the following day. There is a melee in front of the warden's office. The front wheel of the warden's bicycle has been welded at right angles to the frame.

****

Lopa is at IIT for its annual festival. We are at the IIT gate for a meal at the *dhaba*.

Lopa says, 'I didn't know so many IIT guys smoked, Aniket. It seems almost as bad as in Calcutta colleges.'

The Whispered Raga

'Oh, many people who never smoke or listen to rock music are suddenly all over campus doing just that. Especially if there're girls from the "hep" Delhi colleges, like Miranda House, Lady Shriram and so on around. Hey, there's a couple of my wingmates.'

'They look crazy,' says Lopa. 'Why on earth are they running backwards?'

'They're on the campus hockey team. It's an old method for conditioning the leg muscles.'

My wingmates head in our direction. 'Want to do a movie in town guys?' they ask. 'Some guys from the HPS wing have a tempo booked for 8 o'clock.'

****

It is about 1 a.m. later that night. On the return trip, about two miles from the IIT gate, our tempo has stalled. Now there are twenty of us, formerly crammed into a tempo for ten, running back towards campus along the Grand Trunk Road.

We run a little. And then stop to pant and heave and catch our breath. Everyone is cursing the tempo driver.

A truck stops beside us. 'Can I give you a lift?' the driver says in Hindi with a strong Punjabi accent.

Can he! He is a godsend. We clamber aboard post-haste.

****

A two-day festival of classical music organised by the IIT Music Circle is a treat for me and Lopa as we listen to Pandit Bhimsen Joshi and Parween Sultana live for the first time. And the IIT audience, particularly many members of the faculty, are so attentive and discerning.

Parween Sultana has lost her voice. We can barely hear her when she speaks. But when she sings, she effortlessly scales three and a half octaves.

Her Meera *bhajan 'Main to lino Govinda mol, mai ree, main to leeno Govinda mol'* brings tears to the audience's eyes, just as when we listened spellbound to Panditji's *Jo bhaje Hari ko sada* the previous evening.

****

Lopa and I are returning to Calcutta for the Christmas holidays together with two of my wingmates. As usual, we have no reservations.

Short of spending the whole night at the station, it is humanly impossible for us to get them. The first tempo leaves IIT at six in the morning and, after taking a rickshaw from the tempo stand in Kanpur, the very earliest we can make it to the ticket window is six forty-five. By then, the thirteen reserved berths on the Delhi-Calcutta trains are already taken.

We follow our usual course of action. Take the early morning Kalka Mail. The ticket collector throws us off the train at Allahabad. Then take the next local to Mughalsarai. It is a junction station and the railway canteen has delicious chicken and mutton cutlets, even a passable *biryani*. We gorge ourselves and wait for the Bombay Mail. The TT on this train is less strict. We can usually find seats, squeezing in beside various kind souls. In the worst case, if the TT is insistent, there is no other recourse but to pay… But we have not found an alternative in all these years.

TARANA (CRESCENDO)

Calcutta and India, 1996 – 1998

The person of my heart is in my heart

That's why I see her everywhere.

She inhabits the stars in my eyes

That's why she floats away on streams of light.

O that's why I see her here and there

And everywhere I look in any direction.

The person of my heart is in my heart…

— Rabindranath Tagore, after

traditional Baul songs

4.1

It is December 1996, a year after Guruji's death. I am back in Calcutta for the Christmas holidays, as well as the annual festival at the school to be dedicated this year to Guruji's memory.

In one of the school's rehearsal rooms Rita and Lopa are working on a new piece for the upcoming event. Cyrus Madan has come to watch. And I will need to begin serious rehearsals if, after all these years of neglect, I am not to make an onstage spectacle of myself.

Mr. Madan has come up with a novel idea for a piece which will feature several vocalists narrating a story. It is original no doubt, and determinedly contemporary, building on similar efforts on TV but on a larger scale. If it works, the idea will expand to full theatrical pieces, perhaps to be performed with one of the city's leading modern dance or drama companies.

Rita is rehearsing her part in tandem with a young student named Sharmila. She seems to revel in showing off what her student can do for our benefit. Rita never does anything without forethought. Perhaps, she is sending a message to Lopa.

Lopa has been given a small part but has still fared better than Nazrul, who has been left out in the cold. Rita and Sharmila end their piece. 'That's enough for us for today,' Rita says.

Cyrus Madan says, 'How about you going next, Lopa?'

Rita leads her through the piece as Lopa follows a bit hesitantly at first and then as she hits her stride, with her usual fluency.

'No so much flash,' Rita says. 'It's still the middle of the piece and the climax comes later.'

'But I don't know the story. Could you tell me?' Lopa asks.

'Next time. Just follow the piece for today,' Rita replies haughtily.

Lopa's lips tighten. 'I've got it already,' she says. 'See you next time then for the rest. And the story.' This is a new Lopa. I see surprise on Cyrus Madan and Rita's faces as she stomps out of the room.

As she exits, Sureshwari Devi says cuttingly from the corner where she is seated, 'Thinks she's a prima donna. Just like her mother has all her life.'

4.2

I am walking along Rashbehari Avenue towards the bookshops at the Gariahat Road crossing. It is no longer any of my business, but the incident at the school is still playing in my mind.

The streets are emptying out a little, now that the morning office rush is past and it is approaching noon. As I turn left onto Gariahat Road, I see a figure outside the Adi Dhakeshwari Bastralay *sari* store. I recognise Lopa as she turns towards me.

We spend an uncomfortable few minutes browsing in two bookshops, each acutely aware of the presence of the other and the unspoken tension between us. Then we emerge and walk aimlessly along the street sifting through things at some of the hawker's stalls lining the footpath.

Sometime later, we are seated inside a small restaurant named Fantasy just

past Gariahat Market and close to the railway station. It is an old haunt from our school and college days. As we take our seats and order tea, I ask, 'Why did you ask to sit down? To try and explain why things had to be the way they turned out?'

Lopa is silent. Then she quietly says, 'I guess. The last time I tried in Ithaca….' She trails off as she lowers her gaze to the dirty, tiled floor. I notice several strands of grey hair on her head, travelling from her centre parting to the back, like rivulets of glimmering silver in a pool of water by night.

'I'm sober now, unlike then,' I say softly. 'But how does that change anything? If there's anything else besides that you couldn't defy your mother, you can tell me.'

'I'm not sure that I want to…'

The waiter brings the pot of tea, sets it down on the table and leaves.

'But then why even ask to sit down?' I can hear the irritation in my voice.

Her eyes still downcast, she says, 'In Ithaca I saw what's happened to you, Aniket. You wouldn't understand. The hatred in you wouldn't let you.'

'Hatred! What did you expect, brotherly love? Some drivel about how platonic our relationship was, or how amazed I am at your devotion to your mother?' My irritation has given way to a cold fury that even I recognise is unnatural for me. A year ago, I would have attributed it to my alcoholism. Today, I blame Lopa.

'Oh, what's the use, Aniket? I don't know why I'm even trying.'

'Me neither. I see no point in this. And I'll be frank. I do feel resentful every time I see you. I wouldn't go so far as to call it hatred, though.'

Lopa pauses as she seems to gather her thoughts. I expect her to lash back at me, tell me she feels resentful too, but she merely sighs and says, 'Yes, yes. Let's just drop it. Let it be.'

How typical of her! Run from her feelings when matters come to a head. We drink our tea as we descend into our uncomfortable silence once again. I brood while she looks impassive. A young couple emerge from behind the curtains covering the door of one of the stalls. They seem so much in love. How many times have we occupied a stall in this very restaurant! It all seems like it was in some previous lifetime.

'I'm done, Aniket,' Lopa says curtly. I pay the bill and we walk out. 'Which way are you going?' she asks.

'I don't know.' I shrug, trying to be as casual as I can. 'I guess I have time to kill. I'll hang around a bit.' I know where I'm going. I just don't want to be in her presence any longer.

'All right.' See you at the school then.'

'Ya. See you.'

4.3

Nazrul and I have come to the Bakreshwar and Tarapith area, not far from Shantiniketan. It has been one of his regular haunts for many years now. And it feels like a breath of fresh air away from the politics in the school as well as the personal angst that hangs over both of us. Now that I am in Calcutta, at least we have each other to unburden ourselves to.

Nazrul has told me stories about some of his trips to the region and especially about his *moner manush*, whose real name is Mahakal Baba. He is a *tantric sannyasi* but follows some *Baul* rituals as I already know from very our first encounter with him many years ago during the *Poush Mela*.

We visited the main Shiva *mandir* and some of the surrounding temples in Bakreshwar this morning. And bathed in the *dudh* and *agni kundas*, the milk and fire hot springs – two of the ten surrounding the temple complex.

Now we are at the other famous *pith* in the area, the *Tantric* centre of Tarapith. We have made a quick visit to the temple there and then driven through a dark forest to the cremation ground where Mahakal Baba's hut is located in a clearing in the lush banyan grove. It is surrounded by other huts decorated with blood-red skulls. Tridents, snake skins and animal skulls hang from the entrances.

Mahakal Baba is sitting outside his hut surrounded by a group of devotees and visitors. He raises his hand in greeting at Nazrul. Meanwhile, a devotee falls at his feet.

The Whispered Raga

'Why do you keep bothering me?' Mahakal Baba asks the devotee with a touch of irascibility. I learn from Nazrul that this is just his way of avoiding those who've just come to see him out of curiosity.

As the devotee attempts to stutter a reply, Mahakal Baba cuts him short, crying over his words, 'Get lost from here or I'll blind you with these tongs!' He points to the coir glowing in the *dhunuchi* beside him. He picks up a small pebble and pretends to throw it at the devotee.

But the devotee is insistent. 'You must tell me who you are. Tell me, Baba. I've come these many months now. But I won't be turned away this time.'

Mahakal Baba freezes. His anger seems to have evaporated. He peers intently at the man and says in a calm voice, 'D'you know how steep this road is? You must be prepared to give up everything. Can you?'

'With your blessings I'll be able to,' the devotee replies as though in a stupor.

'All right. You see that large stone through the trees? There –,' Baba points with his finger. 'Climb onto it and then jump. Jump right now into the river.'

The devotee runs through the trees and dives straight into the water. The *baba* smiles and turns his attention to me.

I cannot describe what comes over me in that instant. I have never known anything like it, either before or since. It is as though a jolt of lightning has passed through my frame. I too feel like the water is calling out to me. I am possessed by an urge to leave this cremation ground. I feel compelled to let myself afloat on the river.

The *baba* is still smiling his enigmatic smile. 'Go, go, *beta*,' he says, waving me towards the riverbank.

Nazrul waves me on too. 'Don't worry,' he says. 'You can dry your clothes afterwards. *Baba* works in these strange ways.'

I follow the devotee. The water is cool. The moonlight glinting from above casts bewitching ripples in the water. They speak to me in some long forgotten melody. Is this Guruji's whispered *raga*?

I want to explode into laughter – loud, hearty howls of happiness. A great weight lifts off my chest. Now I want to sing. Sing to the stars and the sky above. I have a sense of strength and rejuvenation, like the night Guruji appeared to me in a dream. Ithaca seems so far away now.

The whispered *raga* reveals itself to me at last, like a tempting mistress emerging from the darkness in a misty courtyard. But how had Mahakal Baba known?

4.4

'I want it to be absolutely sold out. And on a scale the school has never done before,' Prem Kishan is saying.

He is on his first visit to Calcutta as co-director of the school and is planning a new format for the annual festival. This 'gala' format is borrowed from New York and will involve many more of the city's glitterati. He has asked me to meet with him and Cyrus Madan to provide some input and feedback on their plans. It seems to me that Nazrul might be a better choice. But I opt for discretion in the matter.

Mr. Madan says, 'Yes, I'm putting out the word across the city through every channel. Mobilising all of our contacts and through ads everywhere. The papers, radio, TV, you name it.'

He seems to be impressed already with Prem Kishan's efforts to cajole and manipulate every member of the school to do whatever they can for the cause.

Others have been observing him as well and not everyone is as sanguine as Cyrus Madan as to how this pushy New York style will fare in an Indian setting. Prem Kishan is certainly leaving no stone unturned in wheedling contributions and scrounging up new sources of support. The concerns are more about his methods and how people in Calcutta's corporate circles might react to them.

'Look!' Prem Kishan says proudly, unrolling a large poster. 'See, Cyrus and Aniket, this is the poster for the very first gala special we did for our school in New York. It was a relatively small affair, nothing like the black tie affairs we've done in recent years.'

The poster is flashy with splotches of colour all over. Loud, I think. Form over matter. Draws attention to itself rather than what it advertises. Not very unlike Prem Kishan himself. 'I think you can do it on a bigger scale here,' I say cautiously. 'Sursagar is already famous, unlike your initial situation in New York. And there are already stars and plenty of high-level social and corporate contacts. The concern, I think, is that the social events not dilute the seriousness of the festival, the actual musical intention of high-level performance and exchange of ideas.'

'How about a really big bash on the final day? After all the music is actually over,' Cyrus Madan says. Prem Kishan rolls up the poster and tucks it away under his arm.

'Yes,' I say. 'That'd be a good compromise. That way, the seriousness of the festival wouldn't be compromised, even if, some people question the need for such a large corporate style bash.'

'In New York, it's like vaudeville. The star performers actually go out of their way to dazzle the crowd. And it's usually spread out throughout the days of the programme.' The enthusiasm in Mr. Madan's voice is so childlike that one would not be mistaken in assuming that he is actually describing his first ever visit to the circus.

'I'm not sure how that would fly here,' I say.

'Well, the purists might complain. They would complain. But it'd probably snare more sponsors,' he says determinedly. Sponsors. Of course. They are all Cyrus Madan lives for.

'We don't have to decide on it today, I suppose,' Prem says. 'But it may be best to not rock the boat too much immediately. Let's think about this, whether to have a sprinkling of social events and mixers throughout the days of the festival. Or one giant bash at the end.'

A well-thought out, reasonable and careful response such as this from Prem is as unlikely as the skies raining gold every monsoon. I am surprised, to say the least.

4.5

I am in one of the small rehearsal rooms of the school, practising my singing intently. Since the encounter with Mahakal Baba, my restlessness has subsided. My passion for music seems to be returning as well, slowly but surely. I have been singing for an hour and a half, something I have not been capable of doing for many months now. But I am still pacing myself gingerly, taking one step at a time and feeling my way forward gradually.

The door of the room opens and Lopa enters. 'The receptionist told me that you were here, Aniket,' she says without any preamble. 'I have to talk to you.' Once again, this seems like a new Lopa.

'I'm all ears.' I lay down my *tanpura*. Perhaps, today she has a retort.

'You've changed, Aniket,' she says as she paces up and down. 'You're not the same person I knew.'

'Are you?' I say, trying to sound flippant 'As I told you before, why should you care? Or anyone else in Calcutta for that matter, now that Guruji's gone. Except for Nazrul, maybe.'

'You're just trying to escape reality. Drown yourself in drink. And denial.'

There it is. The retort. And the accusation. 'I'm sober. Clean as a whistle as the Yanks would say.'

There is a knock on the door and Nazrul enters. 'Ah, Athos and Porthos, I see,' he says. 'D'Artagnan at your service.'

In spite of taking in the lack of amusement on my face he adds, 'An engagement with the Cardinal's guards is at hand, I fear.'

'Oh, cut it out!' Lopa says the words before I can. 'I'm in no mood for it. I was just telling your friend that he's changed.'

'But we all have,' says Nazrul with a sombre nod.

'Yes, but he's just hiding behind self-pity. And drink.'

'I told you in Ithaca,' I say, even more indignantly than before, my teeth gnashing. 'It's my poison of choice.'

'I agree with Lopa, Aniket,' Nazrul says, to my disgust. 'You can't keep escaping reality. That's cowardly.'

'I guess I am a cowardy-custard!' I snap. 'But it's all I have right now, Nazrul. All that gets me through each day. How would you even know what it's like for me in Ithaca? How lonely things can get?'

'Well, I can't actually walk in your shoes, Aniket,' Nazrul says as he backs away from me a few steps. 'But I think I understand. Trust me, things can be pretty darn lonely even when you're surrounded by people, as we always are in India.'

'This isn't leading anywhere. I'm getting by the only way I can, cowardly and escapist as it may seem. I accept that I'm a loser. But thanks for your concern anyway,' I add with as much sarcasm as I can muster.

'Ah, now you really sound so formal, so American,' Nazrul says with a slight twinkle.

'When in Rome...' I snort. 'Otherwise, as I told you guys, you have your head sheared and spend your days in sackcloth and ashes.'

4.6

We are at the school watching a full rehearsal of the novel story piece featuring the group of singers.

Rita is dressed to kill today, unnecessary and out of place for a daytime rehearsal. From where I am sitting, I can hear her whispered comments to her student Sharmila. She is pointing out some finer points on the parts Sharmila will be singing.

For a moment, I feel sympathetic towards Lopa who is sitting quietly in a corner. Rita is sure to make Sharmila a star and sabotage Lopa in the process. Like Sureshwari Devi and Idanbai all over again. This eternal clawing for fame. I feel a perverse pleasure at the thought of this, but the next instant it is replaced by a sense of shame, almost of guilt.

As good as Sharmila is, she strains every sinew to keep up with Rita's brilliance this morning. Rita is giving it her all today, singing as though it is show time already. Perhaps, she is trying to cement her status before the new co-director. As though she has read my mind from a distance she leans over towards Prem Kishan and exchanges some words and a smile with him. It feels depressing, this scrambling for position and power.

Nazrul walks into the room. Rita doesn't even acknowledge him as he takes a seat beside me. Instead, she goads Sharmila to one final brilliant movement and then turns towards Mr. Madan and Prem with a bow and a flourish of her outstretched hands. She certainly knows how to play to the gallery, to graciously emphasise that

Sharmila's performance is really her doing. This process of music making and breaking stars – it's an eternal round.

Now Rita leans over towards Prem and Cyrus Madan. Her sari slips off her shoulder. Nazrul stiffens a bit beside me as she is all over Prem Kishan for the next few minutes. Perhaps there is more to her dress and demeanour than I have suspected.

It is Lopa's turn now, but it seems that Rita has set up the scene to her own ends. She certainly knows all the tricks of the trade. Nazrul watches impassively as she reproduces the deliberate bossiness and non-cooperation of the previous rehearsal with Lopa.

Lopa is still uncertain of the exact place of her pieces in the overall story. Rita turns towards Prem Kishan and Cyrus Madan periodically, as if to emphasise Lopa's lack of fluency and the obvious contrast to Rita and Sharmila's part.

When rehearsal is over, Cyrus Madan and Prem dive deep into conversation with Rita. She nuzzles up next to Prem Kishan. Her hand rests on his forearm and her cleavage peeps out again. When they are done, Cyrus Madan and Rita sweep past Lopa without a word. Only Prem turns to say goodbye to her.

4.7

The next morning, as Nazrul and I walk into the rehearsal room, Rita and Cyrus Madan are talking to Lopa. 'You don't need me then?' Lopa says.

There is no reply from either Rita or Cyrus. After a long pause, Lopa adds, 'I think Sharmila can do my part perfectly. She's very talented obviously.'

'Since we're on the topic,' Cyrus Madan says in a syrupy sweet voice, 'I just wanted to also tell you that you'll be singing on the very last evening this time, Lopa.'

I am tempted to intervene but I hold my tongue.

****

After they leave the room, Nazrul puts his hand on Lopa's shoulders. She turns from the window to look at us. Her eyes are wet.

'I'm very sorry about all of this,' Nazrul says. 'Really, Lopa.'

'I know, Nazrul,' she says. There is a catch in her voice. 'I just wonder what I should do once *Ammi*...' She bites her lip.

'I'm very sorry too,' I say. 'Should I say something to Prem? Or Cyrus Madan?' I did not want to intervene before, but I am more than willing now to say something. Perhaps there is some truth in what Lopa and Nazrul say of me – that I am a coward.

'Thanks, Aniket. I thought that you might enjoy seeing me in this state,' Lopa says.

'Now, come on, Lopa. I haven't sunk that low!' I say. 'Even though, to quote you, I'm a cowardly escapist and alcoholic. But really, should I speak to them?'

'It wouldn't make an iota of difference,' she says as she chokes back a sob. 'Just cause a rift between you and them.'

'I guess you're right.'

'Of course she's right!' Nazrul says. 'They make a pretty pair, Madan and my darling wife. Made for each other. They'd win the Wills couples contest hands down,' he adds cuttingly. He then laughs – the harsh, ironic rasp I previously heard in Ithaca. 'The eternal dance of the sexes. Prem Kishan and Rita. I think she's set her cap for him. And she doesn't even bother to hide it anymore.'

Lopa is silent. I am embarrassed, feeling his hurt. To change the subject, I say, 'Ya. They're quite a threesome, I suppose.'

'Oh yes. They'll convert the school to a three-ring circus before long,' Nazrul says.

Lopa turns back to the window, staring into the distance once again. 'How about we show them?' she says quietly. 'We could do it, right?'

Does she mean revenge? Showing them up? Exposing them? Either way, I am impressed with her audacity. 'Now this is a new Lopa,' I say. 'One I like much better.'

'Hey, cut it out the two of you. Quit sparring. What can't the three musketeers do if we put our heads together?' says Nazrul.

4.8

It is the penultimate evening of the festival. Everything so far has gone according to Mr. Madan's plans. Rita's recital and her performance with Sharmila in the experimental piece have received rave reviews. Niloy has also outdone himself the previous evening. Today will be the *piece de resistance*, the joint performance which will establish Rita and Niloy as the undisputed stars in the school's new pecking order.

They begin their set pieces slowly before proceeding to the famous *Tori gaili gaili endi endi phirat sub nari* in *raga Vasant*. Near the end, as they move into the lightning-paced *taans* for which both are already celebrated, they keep casting meaningful glances at Nazrul and me in the audience. There is no little challenge in their gazes.

****

At our request, Cyrus Madan has been only too happy to move Nazrul's performance back to the last evening where Lopa and mine were already scheduled to be. No doubt, he expects the brouhaha surrounding the gala on the last day to take the focus away from our singing, thus killing two stars with one stone.

As in the past, both Lopa and Nazrul are supposed to take everything he throws at them lying down. Cyrus Madan has really been asking for it, some really strong medicine for a very long time now.

On this final evening, the glitterati of Calcutta society are swarming around the club where the reception for this new gala event is being held. The school has never before hosted a social event on this scale. In spite of my misgivings about how his style of business might transplant to Calcutta, Prem Kishan has done his job well, far exceeding even Mr. Madan's wildest expectations.

I see Nazrul emerging from a group in the far corner of the room and walk over to him. 'Nervous?' he asks.

I nod and wipe my sweaty palms on my trousers. It is my first performance on a big stage in a long time – fifteen years, to be precise. The crowd is electric. I never imagined something on this scale and before every VIP in town. One mistake and the critics will skewer me.

'Everything'll be fine,' Nazrul attempts to assuage my fears. 'Do the breath and concentration exercises and then give it your all. We'll take 'em by storm like in the old days. Boldness above all.'

Downstairs, the lobby is full of guests. At the bottom of the broad staircase, a red velvet rope is periodically being lifted for the VIPs who have been issued the gilt-edged invitation cards. The ticket prices they have paid through their noses will keep Mr. Madan in the pink for many months to come.

There is generous applause as Rita Mahalanobis and Sureshwari Devi make their entrance. They are careful to artlessly keep their distance from us as the guests cluster all around them.

Prem Kishan and Mr. Madan approach Nazrul and me. 'Would you like to welcome the guests at the entrance for some time?' Prem asks me.

'In a while,' I say as I watch Lopa enter the room. She waves at us and walks over. We talk for a while, periodically waving to someone or pausing as people stop by to chat.

After some more time, as we take fresh drinks and go out onto the verandah,

Rita joins us. I am just about to leave to welcome guests at the entrance when

Prem Kishan says, 'Hey, today's your big night guys, all three of you. All pumped up?'

'We'll see,' I say offhandedly. 'After this bash, I'm not sure how much concentration will be left for the music.' Mr. Madan smiles weakly.

'Oh, I'm sure there'll be some serious listeners in the audience,' Rita says patronisingly. Her comment would otherwise anger me, but tonight I am too nervous to take offense at her pettiness. Turning to Lopa she says very sweetly, 'Perhaps you can rehearse properly with us next time. The VIPs and papers are all raving about our experimental piece, you know.' The smile congeals on Lopa's face.

'I'd better go experiment at the entrance,' I say, hoping to break the tension. 'Might snare the rest of the VIPs and press corps!' Rita glares at me but I am off before she can respond.

****

It is later in the evening at the Kala Mandir where the festival is being held this year to accommodate the record crowds. The master of ceremonies has just announced that the three of us will be performing together. Surprise is writ large on Mr. Madan's face but it is too late. Even if he wishes to, he cannot stop us anymore.

We take our places onstage and Nazrul's *swar-mandal* and our *tanpura*s are tuned to the *sarangi* and the *tabla*s. Nazrul begins by softly humming the *pakad* of *raga Vasant*. Lopa and I join in as he proceeds to Guruji's famous *vilambit alaap* and *khayal* in *raga Vasant*. Half an hour later, the smug smiles have disappeared from the faces of yesterday's star duo. Mr. Madan too is now scowling.

But we are not done yet. Nazrul smiles at me as we conclude the piece. No words are exchanged but Lopa and I switch smoothly to the same *Tori gaili gaili endi endi phirat sub nari* that Rita and Niloy performed the previous evening.

The scowls on their faces have now darkened to pure anger. This is a contravention of the most sacrosanct of all musical etiquette. And before this audience of VIPs!

As we continue past the magical melodic variations in the ultra-high registers, Lopa inclines her head slightly. We explode into *taans, paltas* and *sargams*, but with the restraint and sweetness on which Idanbai and Guruji have always placed the greatest emphasis.

An elegantly dressed lady in the first row turns to her neighbour and says quite audibly, 'How much more satisfying this is than yesterday!'

As I take a quick *phirat* at the upper register and come to rest at the tonic,

Nazrul bursts into Abdul Karim Khan's famous *Pilu thumri 'Soch samajh naadaan'*. We can no longer even hear ourselves amidst the bursts of applause.

Half an hour later, as we stand up to leave the stage, the hall is rent by renewed cries, this time of, '*Aar ekta, aar ekta! Ek aur, ek aur!* Once more, please!'

We exchange questioning glances and then, as the insistent cries continue, we sit back down. We anticipated this call for encore even before our recital began.

This time, Lopa and Nazrul follow up a very short *alaap* by a *mukhda* leading into the spectacular *tarana*. The brilliant juxtapositions of Farsi verses or *bayets* from Nazrul are punctuated by Lopa's couplets from Jayadeva's Sanskrit *ashtapadi* poetry in the Gwalior style. Together with fast variations of beat at each transition, they once again bring the audience to their feet in a rousing finale.

****

'Aniket, will you come and see *Ammi*? Please. She's been asking to see you ever since she heard you were coming too. I've just been afraid to ask you till today.' The note of entreaty in Lopa's voice is very marked.

Now that the bulk of the audience has left, we are standing outside the large marquee, savouring the success of a plan only two weeks in the implementation but really many years in the making. Mr. Madan has stalked past us on his way out.

The Whispered Raga

I try to gauge the avalanche of feelings which Lopa's question has triggered in my mind, even after the high I am still feeling from the performance. Finally, I say, 'Could Nazrul go with me? I'd feel much better if he did.'

As Lopa considers my request Nazrul breaks in, 'Idanbai's on her deathbed, Aniket. The doctors say she's getting uraemia and will slide into a coma soon. This is between you and her. You should go alone. And soon. Before it's too late.'

My eyes flit from one face to another. 'All right,' I say with a sigh. 'I'll come tomorrow morning. Would ten o'clock be a good time?'

4.9

Idanbai is lying on the bed. She seems curiously shrivelled up and bent. Only her eyes show signs of alertness. She tries to smile as I touch her feet in greeting but the pain contorts her features into a grimace.

We sit silently for some time. I look at those lovely features now collapsed inwards like a death's head. There has always been an unspoken silence between us ever since I have grown to adulthood. A palpable but unarticulated tension. But it is gone today.

I have been unsure of what my feelings will be on seeing Idanbai, whether the anger and hurt of so many dark years might come bubbling to the surface. But I feel only pity as I see the tears glistening in her eyes.

She clasps my hand and blubbers, 'Please forgive me! Please forgive me, *beta*.'

I am unsure of how to respond. 'There's nothing to forgive Idanbai – I mean, auntie,' I say sheepishly. 'It almost killed me though.'

The tears stream from her eyes. 'I never gave you a chance,' she says. 'It was my fear. Fear of society. Of our past.' She breaks into a coughing fit. She is already tiring.

After the spasms of coughing have passed she adds, 'I didn't realise how faithful you could be, though Vishnu tried to tell me. "It will kill him," he told me. "That boy is a person of deep feelings and deep loyalties. He'll never get over it."'

'You know, auntie, love is a sign. A code, a recognition of some deep inner affinity. Some fellowship of the soul, isn't it? A compass pointing you to your true north, Guruji once said.' Second-hand wisdom is all I have to offer Idanbai at this time.

'Yes, *beta*. And perhaps music tunes souls even more finely. Even more closely together. But my fear didn't let me admit that till it was too late. Even though I knew it. And sang about it every single day of my life.'

Tears stream down Lopa's cheeks. 'You almost killed me too, *Ammi*,' she says, gently stroking her mother's limp hair.

Idanbai raps her knuckles feebly on her forehead again and again in a mute gesture of contrition. Her crossed hands in front of her emaciated face look pitiable. She pulls Lopa to her breast and says, 'I know, *beti*. Due to my stupidity, I've watched you die a little bit more every single time you visited Calcutta. Withering away like an untended, unloved, unfed vine.' She is crying more profusely, the sobs racking her shrunken frame. 'How could I see it and not die inwardly myself? Not curse myself every waking moment for my stupid folly?'

We sit in silence for a long time until Idanbai breaks the hush. 'D'you see the fish in the aquarium?' she says. 'Aren't the swishing tails sounding *raga Desi Todi*, exactly the *ma-pa-re-ga-sa-re-ni-sa*?'

I am startled. Is she delirious? But she is smiling peacefully for the first time today.

I blurt out, 'Lopa, why didn't you marry? You know, the senior student at the Bhatkhande College. Or someone else? I'm sure you had no dearth of suitors.'

Lopa is silent. After a minute, Idanbai takes Lopa's hand in hers and says, 'Don't you see, *beta*? You should have known that she was even more loyal than you. She never even looked at anyone else.'

Then she takes my hand too and puts it on Lopa's, saying, '*Beta*, my time has come. Take her, *beta*. I leave her in your care. Make her happy, *beta*. She has been starved for so long due to my foolish stubbornness.'

As we sit silently, she adds, 'It was my fondest wish that I would sing at Lopa's wedding. But that is not to be. I've left it far too late. But here is a tape I have recorded for the two of you. Remember me by it.'

I sit down on the bed next to Lopa, stroking Idanbai's hair too. 'Oh, *Ammi*,' I say, 'Can I call you that? I so wanted to, instead of always saying auntie.'

As she smiles at me, I add, 'I was always so scared of returning to India, of opening the wound deeper than I dared. But I'm free now. I realise that, I just realised it. We will be married today, right now, *Ammi*.'

4.10

Lopa and I are in western India for our honeymoon. We have returned to Bombay after visiting the Ajanta and Ellora caves and the stunning complex of over a thousand exquisitely sculpted Jain temples in Palitana.

We are sitting in the hotel room listening to the necklace of *thumris*, treasures gleaned over a lifetime from now lost sources which Idanbai has lovingly gifted to us. Marriage, I realise now, suits me so far. More so with Lopa. The restlessness, the uneasiness that has been clawing away at my sanity has begun to ebb away. I smile more now, snap a little less. Lopa and I are not the teenaged or twenty-something lovers we once were, but our feelings for each other have remained unchanged – only grown stronger through the years of separation.

Unseasonably for winter, it begins to rain. 'Aniket, I want to go to the seaside,' says Lopa.

'All right. We'll get a cab and go once the rain stops.'

'No, no. I want to go right now. My mind's dancing. I want to visit the seaside in the rain.'

It is almost lunchtime and I am hungry but I don't waste any more words. We have a lifetime ahead of us to haggle over the tiny details. So I call a cab and ask the driver to take us to the seaside. He seems puzzled but drives us anyway, chattering away all the way to Marine Drive. We stop at the cemented entrance of a public beach. The driver telegraphs his thoughts in no uncertain manner as we step out into the pouring rain and I pay the fare.

Lopa takes me by the hand and we walk a short distance on the beach. Then she motions and says, 'Let's sit, Aniket.'

'What, here? On the sand? But everything's wet.'

Giggling, she pulls me down beside her. We watch the rain coming down in torrents while the waves crash into the concrete seawall and careen off high into the air like a huge fountain. 'I feel like singing,' Lopa suddenly says, breaking into a *mukhda* for *raga Malhar*.

As each giant wave leaps into the air, Lopa's *taans* follow them, now into the ultra-high registers and then down to the deepest bass. Like Nazrul's *Jogiya* in the Khoyai, those long years ago, I find myself transfixed in some other ether, somewhere between the earth and sky.

I do not know how long we sit in this way, but the next thing I remember is us walking arm-in-arm, singing Tagore's *Mamo chitte, niti nritte, ke je nache, ta-ta thai thai, ta-ta thai thai* – 'Who is this incessantly dancing *ta-ta thai thai* in my heart?'

We sit down again on the wet sand. Lopa pulls me to her and breaks into Tagore's *Kobe tumi ashbe bolo* – 'Tell me when you'll come'. We sing at the tops of our voices, embellishing the melody with whatever flourishes and ornaments we please. We sing to the wind and the waves. Tears stream from both our eyes.

The whispered *raga* reveals itself to me once again.

4.11

We are back at the hotel. Mr. Madan has left a message from Calcutta. We need to call him back urgently.

An hour later, we are on our way to Bombay Airport. Rita and Prem Kishan have eloped! And Nazrul has attempted suicide.

On the phone, Cyrus Madan seemed crushed, ready to melt into the earth with guilt and shame. He blamed himself for having brought this on the school by cultivating Prem Kishan's appointment as co-director. I tried to console him, saying, 'If it's meant to be, it can't be stopped, Cyrus.'

'Stuff and nonsense,' he responded with a flash of his usual manner. 'What fatalism, utter balderdash'.

Lopa and I are silent as the taxi enters the main gate at Sahar Airport. It is not just the shock. The same Rita whose elopement with Nazrul so many years ago caused the first break in our relations has done it again. What more might we not see in our lifetimes!

****

Nazrul is lying on the bed, his face wan and pinched. He looks tired but he smiles as Lopa, Cyrus Madan and I enter his cabin at the Bellevue Nursing Home. The nurse warns us, 'He's still very weak. Don't tire him out too much.'

Words would be meaningless anyway, but Nazrul seems strangely buoyant, almost radiant. Happier than we have seen him in many months.

'Where's *Ammi*?' he asks.

'She's in shock, Nazrul,' I say. 'She blames herself. And what she calls "that scheming, gold-digging Rita."' She also said, 'Our sins are being visited on my son,' but I think this is hardly the time to tell Nazrul that.

Nazrul appears not even to notice what I say or at least doesn't make any acknowledgement. He seems to have slipped back into a reverie with his eyes fixed at a distant point outside the window. Perhaps it is just the effect of the drugs he has been administered.

Just as we are about to leave, he says, 'D'you know what happened?'

'What d'you mean?' Lopa asks. 'What happened when?'

'After I took the poison,' Nazrul replies. 'I dreamt of Mahakal Baba.'

'So,' I say. 'It isn't the first time.'

'Ah, but listen to what happened after that. After they woke me up, and they say it was a miracle that I even survived, another Nazrul, a sitar maker from Chetla, came rushing into the school. He too had dreamt of Mahakal Baba. And had been instructed in his dream to come to the school to see me.'

'What!' Cyrus Madan cries.

'Yes,' Nazrul says sanguinely. 'We talked and decided that he should go and meet Mahakal Baba in his ashram at Tarapith.'

'And?' Lopa says.

'As soon as Mahakal Baba saw the man entering his hut, he began yelling. "Tell that imbecile who bears your name, go tell him that he has no right to take his own life. He still has work left to do and then he can die in peace. Tell him that the blessings of Allah will rain down on him."'

****

Later that evening, Lopa and I visit Sureshwari Devi in her flat. We are ushered by a servant into her bedroom.

In the darkness, I make her out beckoning us to sit beside her on the bed. She looks distraught and unkempt, almost like the mad women that one sometimes sees roaming the streets.

She draws us both into an embrace and cries out, 'Forgive me! Forgive me! Tell Idanbai, Lopa. Please tell her that it's all my fault. Tell her that I beg her on my hands and knees to forgive me. It's my pride which caused this. Only my pride!'

We sit there, frozen in shock for a minute, as she repeatedly strikes her head on the headboard. I step in, and Lopa draws Sureshwari Devi tightly to her breast and tries to hold her there. They struggle and then she sinks limply onto the bed. I feel my hands clench into fists as her sobs rent the darkened room.

4.12

December 1997. Lopa and I are back in Calcutta again for Idanbai's last rites. Afterwards, Lopa will visit Bhatkhande College for a few days, as we have decided she should on each of our visits to India. A chastened Mr. Madan has graciously offered to host her at the Sursagar School for the rest of our trip.

Nazrul and I will accompany Mahakal Baba on a tour of some holy sites in central India. We will travel through the Vindhya mountain range.

****

The stars are shining above us tonight, peering faintly through the deepening gloom of the December evening. The dense darkness all around us seems to have congealed even more thickly today in the freezing cold of the Amarkantak mountains, the source of the Narmada river. It is spreading like an inky blanket over the forests and valleys covering the Vindhya range.

Another procession of ash-smeared, naked and half-clothed *sannyasis* wends its way down the Amarkantak mountainside. 'Seeing them, seeing all of this, I feel a sudden whim. Why not just go off with them?' Nazrul says wistfully.

I smile. 'You're a free man now. Remember you once told me that you could say that the whole world is your oyster because you'd gone to a convent school?'

He smiles too and says, 'And now it really is, isn't it? At least we'll taste the flavour of life in the wild a little. Real freedom.'

****

We have been travelling for some days. The Narmada, bloated by countless mountain streams, cascades down the hillsides as we navigate along its banks. Like us, there are other groups of pilgrims and *sannyasis* covering the terrain on foot. Each day, we walk through the forest and the sandy bars along the river banks till the next temple or place of rest.

But some strange addiction seems to have gripped Nazrul. As the days go by, the river and its surrounding terrain seem to exert an increasingly hypnotic draw on him. In the past few days, there has been an astonishing transition in his dress and demeanour, even more so than after Rita's elopement with Prem Kishan.

He walks every day in the same shirt and the same pair of trousers, oblivious to my entreaties. They are streaked with dirt and have begun to resemble the torn attire of a hippie or ruffian. His beard and moustache cover his face like undergrowth.

We have walked for almost ten days now. My enthusiasm is as high as ever, but the physical strain has begun to tell on me. Nazrul's stamina, however, is astonishing. He shows no sign of tiredness. He has never been athletic. But now it is as if he is driven by some stream of joy and limitless strength.

I feel apprehensive about directly questioning Mahakal Baba. But what is this new state Nazrul is in? He is almost unaware of reality, disconnected from or strangely apathetic to our surroundings.

****

It is now our last evening. We are sitting around a fire on the riverbank. Nazrul is singing, humming quietly to himself. He seems aware of us today once again, of our environs. He has been intently observing a flock of birds wheeling around in the sky.

Mahakal Baba tells me with a smile, 'Your friend is lucky indeed. The joy that is flowing into his life is hard for most people to attain or bear. It is all *leela*. From now, he will be ensnared in a web of sound.'

'The whispered *raga*!' I exclaim.

Mahakal Baba's smile widens.

4.13

Some months later, Lopa and I are again back in Calcutta for the summer holidays.

Nazrul and the two of us are sitting on one of the verandahs wrapping round the school courtyard one morning when a postman hands us a letter. 'It's from the US,' Nazrul says. 'Wonder who it could be? Oh, it's from our friend Prem Kishan,' he adds, gritting his teeth. 'How dare he? He has the gall to write. After what he did!'

'Here, let me read it,' Lopa says, hastily taking it from his hand. 'I know that I have grievously wronged you, Nazrul,' she begins reading. 'I only hope that you have begun to find peace in your heart and that someday you will find the strength to forgive us.

'I have news too. Things have not gone well between Rita and me from the very beginning. Last week, we went to visit the Glacier National Park on the US-Canada border for the 4th of July holiday. It was a breath-taking place. As we drove up the 'Highway to Heaven' with the giant glaciers falling away on all sides, it felt like we really were suspended between the earth and sky. Like the spectacular scenery all around Yudhisthira as he loses Draupadi and his brothers one by one during their final journey to the otherworld in the *Mahabharata*.

'But it was too good to last. As we pitched camp that afternoon near one of the trails far from the main road, we began bickering again. In a fit of anger, I yelled at Rita, accusing her of flirting with a musician from the New York Philharmonic who has been working with us on an

East-meets-West project. This has been a continuing bone of contention these past months.

'Rita, temperamental as always, ran off. I could tell that she had no sense of where she was going. I stood there petrified for some minutes, too dazed to even register what had occurred in the wink of an eye.

I saw Rita walking over a small rope bridge clearly marked "Keep Off". Her steps were unsteady. And her body was swaying. I yelled out at the top of my voice, "Rita, stop! Stop for God's sake. Be careful."

'I could clearly see her climbing the steep rocky road on the far side of the warning sign. Even from the distance, I could make out that her whole body was trembling.

'I ran after her with a jackhammer pounding in my stomach. One tiny misstep or a loose foothold! And as the thought flashed through my mind, I saw her slip as a cloud of debris and falling rock rose all around. And then, before my horrified gaze, she hurtled straight into the ravine on the far side.

'I have been absolved of all blame after the enquiry. But what have I done?! What made me say those words? A moment's slip of the tongue after months of restraint. How could I ever have done it?

The park rangers consoled me by saying, 'It's not your fault. She was an adult after all.'

'But Nazrul, how will I make you understand? How can I forgive myself? I feel like I'm crucified by guilt every waking moment, suspended right there between the earth and sky on that Highway to Heaven.'

As Lopa finishes reading, Nazrul gasps in shock. I remember it too – the face-reader's words from all those long years ago! We sit in stunned, shocked silence, as the scene from so many years ago unspools in my mind's eye.

****

Is there a design in such things? Some flow of energy, of some mysterious life force, perhaps what people term destiny. Are we marionettes in the hands of some master puppeteer? Or merely random waves in an ocean of chance?

****

After what seems an eternity, Lopa breaks the silence, 'Poor Rita,' she says.

'Poor Prem,' she adds as though he is an afterthought. 'He'll be tormented all his life.'

Nazrul has been looking down at his feet, 'Yes,' he says. 'I don't think I can feel anger at him any more you know. Although it's hard for me to forgive Rita.

You know, she didn't even look after her father when he was on his deathbed.'

'I didn't know that,' I say. 'If this hadn't happened, even half an hour ago, I'd have been glad to declare Rita a real bitch. But I don't think I'd go so far as to say she got what was coming to her.'

'Come on, Aniket,' Lopa says, coming up to me and putting her hand on my shoulder. 'Be charitable. Remember the dream involving Guruji which you've been having. Let it all go. Just forgive and forget.'

'What's that, now?' Nazrul says. 'You've been dreaming about Guruji?'

I wonder how best to tell him. 'Have you seen the movie *Places in the Heart*, Nazrul?' I say. Nazrul shakes his head. So I tell him about it. I tell him that it is the story of a woman, played by Sally Field, whose sheriff husband is accidentally killed by a drunken black boy. How members of the KKK then lynch the boy and drive away a black man who's been helping her. And how another character in the movie has an affair with her friend.

'But what's all this got to do with you or with Guruji?' Nazrul asks. 'D'you mean the guy having an affair a la Rita and Prem?'

'No,' I say, 'Hang on.' I tell him that what I've been seeing in my dreams is the final scene of the movie which takes place in a church. As the preacher speaks, and he always has Guruji's face, the adulterer's wife takes his hand for the first time since his affair, and the man feels the overwhelming power of forgiveness. Guruji points to him from the pulpit. Wine for the communion is then passed around. As each person drinks, he or she says, 'Peace of God.' And when Sally Fields drinks that wine, her dead sheriff husband appears right beside her. He drinks from the goblet and Guruji walks down from his pulpit and blesses him. Then Guruji walks over to the black boy who had killed the sheriff by accident and holds the cup as the boy drinks and says 'Peace of God.'

'Yes, *bhai*,' he says softly after I finish narrating. 'Lopa's right. I think Guruji's telling you to forgive and forget.' He hesitates and then adds, 'Maybe he's trying to tell all of us.'

Forgiveness. A small word with a large heart. I have often wondered whether I am magnanimous enough to embrace it and let it flow unhindered through me. My bitterness has corroded me, acid-washed my emotions through the years to the point of leaving me brittle. I am tired. Perhaps it is time to commence on that arduous path to forgiveness, to mending what has been broken.

I see a small sign Sursagar School of Music peeping at me from the corner of one of the ground-floor corridors wrapping around school. Perhaps it is the ocean of music that needs to wash freely over all of us again.

'Come, come to your brother,' Nazrul says through his outstretched hands. That road will not be easy, but with him and Lopa by my side, at least I will not be alone. He gathers us into a giant bear hug. It is a long time before we break free.

NOTES AND ACKNOWLEDGEMENTS

The characters and events in this book are entirely fictitious. However, there are some incidents drawn from life, particularly those involving Dadu, but modified to the needs of the story.

One of my goals was to try and tell a dramatic story set within the world of north Indian classical music. In re-creating this world, my debt to the three Bengali books by the well-known vocalist, musicologist and author Pandit Kumarprasad Mukhopadhyay is hard to overstate.

Of them, *Kudrat Rangibirangi* is simply the best book of its kind I know. Its combination of erudition and intimate experience of the world of north Indian classical music spanning two generations, juxtaposed with a rare confluence of head and heart that informs every page, make it a true classic of its kind. And *Majlish* and *Mehfil*, while written in a very different, raconteur style, round out the picture by providing personal details and charming anecdotes about many great north Indian classical musicians, warts and all.

Almost all the stories about the music world of olden days, which are recounted here are taken from the books above. And some incidents narrated in the books have also been given a dramatic, modified, fictional treatment in my storyline. In particular, attentive and knowledgeable readers will recognise mystical incidents drawn from the life of the great genius Ustad Abdul Karim Khan.

One scene is also very loosely based on a chapter in the Bengali book, *Sadhu Sant-er Moha Shongome* by Shankar Nath Roy.

My debt to my own Dadu in introducing me to north Indian classical music is, as with many other things, beyond words. If this book succeeds in showing the endless richness of this world even a little, especially as manna for the soul and as a staff of life, then it will have been more than worth the effort that went into the writing. As it is, the process of researching and weaving the story has been a great source of pleasure to me over the past months.

I owe a very special debt of thanks to my editor at BecomeShakespeare, Aparna Sundaresan, for her meticulous attention to the manuscript, including numerous suggestions, which have improved it immeasurably. Besides her, my sincere gratitude is due to Urvi Dutt for producing a beautiful cover design, which I loved right away, Niyati Joshi for casting the cover blurb into its present intriguing form, and for overall editorial oversight. My thanks also to Pallavi Borkar for guiding the entire process of getting the book from its raw stages to what you hold in your hand.

I would never have had the courage and persistence to complete this book without the constant support and prodding of my darling daughter and wife Maya and Marianna, and periodic words of wisdom and encouragement from my brother-in-law Purnendu Roy and his team at Orion Entertainment in Calcutta. And last, but certainly not the least, I would never have attempted any sort of creative writing at all but for my late father's prodding. His spirit seems to have watched over this effort as well.

As to craft, the sage advice and hands-on instruction of a couple of Hollywood scriptwriting gurus in particular has been invaluable, going far deeper than the best creative writing classes anywhere.

ABOUT THE AUTHOR

Sudipto Roy Choudhury holds a BTech in engineering from IIT Kanpur and a PhD in mathematical physics from Cornell University, as well as a certificate on screen and novel writing from the Hollywood Screenwriters' Guild.

His published literary work includes the novel *I Shall Come Out as a Tremendous Comet* (Rupa, 2009) and two volumes of translated short stories – *The Arabian Nights of Kolkata and Other Stories* (Calcutta Writers' Workshop, 2002) and *Prometheus Unbound: Short Stories of Samaresh Basu* (Rupa, 2006). He also has 97 published research articles in top journals in mathematical physics and was founding Chair of the Society of Industrial and Applied Mathematics Activity Group on Nonlinear Waves and Coherent Structures. He teaches at the University of Central Florida in Orlando, USA and can be reached at roy.choudhury141@gmail.com. He has also written miscellaneous columns on film in *The Hindu* (Madras) and *The Statesman* (Calcutta), and articles in *World Literature Today, Asian Affairs* et cetera. Among them was a monthly column on European art film which ran in *The Statesman* from 1992 to 1998.

www.ingramcontent.com/pod-product-compliance
Lightning Source LLC
Chambersburg PA
CBHW022110040426
42450CB00006B/654